MAKE YOUR
FIRST
MILLION
IN NETWORK
MARKETING

MAKE YOUR
FIRST
MILLION
IN NETWORK
MARKETING

Proven Techniques
You Can Use to Achieve
Financial Success

Mary Christensen
with **Wayne Christensen**

Adams Media Corporation
Avon, Massachusetts

For Nikki and David, Beki and Dane.

Published by
Adams Media, an F+W Publications Company
57 Littlefield Street, Avon, MA 02322. U.S.A.
www.adamsmedia.com

ISBN 10: 1-58062-482-0
ISBN 13: 978-1-58062-482-4
Printed in Canada.

J I H G

Library of Congress Cataloging-in-Publication Data
Christensen, Mary.
Make your first million in network marketing / by Mary Christensen
with Wayne Christensen.
p.   cm.
ISBN 1-58062-482-0
1. Multilevel marketing. I Christensen, Wayne.
HF 5415.126 C488   2001
658.8'4--dc21   00-065006

This book is available for quantity discounts for bulk purchases.
For information, call 1-800-289-0963.

ACKNOWLEDGMENTS

Thanks to Edward W. Knappman of New England Publishing Associates and Adams Media Corporation for their confidence in supporting a new author; to my husband, Wayne, without whose help this would never have been written; and to Nigel Sinclair, for being my mentor.

CONTENTS

PART SEVEN: *MILLION-DOLLAR LEADERSHIP* ... 179

PART ONE

Own Your

Own Business,

Own Your

Own Life

CHAPTER 1

Is Network Marketing Right for You?

This is a book about you. You're probably reading it because you're already in network marketing and want to know how to achieve more success and achieve your success more quickly and more easily.

Or perhaps someone has tried to recruit you, talking about an opportunity everyone except you seems to be actively involved in. Naturally, you're curious, even a little skeptical, about the truth behind the claims of this seemingly magical way of making money.

Alternatively, you may want to know how you can become successfully self-employed, breaking away from the nine-to-five routine that you feel is robbing you of your life.

Whether you want to bring extra dollars into your household income every week, fit a career into your family life, or work from home and make the kind of income you secretly dream of but have never believed to be possible for you, you'll find answers in this book.

People who say you can make a million dollars overnight in network marketing are talking hype, not substance. You can become a millionaire in this industry, but you will never make it without adopting two principles—and using them every day of your life.

The first is to pay consistent attention to your business. In other words, you can make a million dollars and more, but you will have to work for it.

The second, and most important, is to develop your ability to help other people become successful. More than anything else, this will determine the speed at which you make your first million.

What Is Network Marketing?

In its early days, network marketing was the darling of wildly enthusiastic entrepreneurs. And it still is. Today, however, some of the original companies are traded publicly on the New York Stock Exchange and NASDAQ, and blue-chip *Fortune* 500 companies are incorporating network marketing into their corporate strategies, endorsing it as a sound, strong, and successful way of doing business.

Recent years have brought dramatic changes in people's lifestyles. Companies are downsizing, cities are becoming more congested, and values are changing. Two-income families are the norm rather than the exception. More and more people are making a lifestyle choice, closing the door on a corporate career and beginning to enjoy the quality of life available when working from home. The momentum of urban drift continues, leaving rural areas underserviced in retail choices.

And although network marketing is not dependent upon e-commerce, the dot-com revolution has made dramatic changes to the way all business is conducted.

All of these developments bring ever increasing opportunities for people in the network marketing industry to sell direct to friends, family, and neighbors. Thus it has become easier for millions of men and women of all ages, educational levels, and backgrounds to succeed as independent salespeople.

This way of selling is variously known as network marketing, multi-level marketing, direct selling, and relationship marketing. Sometimes the companies involved give their system of selling other names, such as "Party Plan" and "Show Plan."

Network marketing is built on a foundation of direct selling. Some think of it as a new way of doing things. But direct selling is simply and primarily the business of selling a product or service face to face, away from a fixed retail location. It's the way business has been conducted since the beginning of time. It gives you the opportunity to be "in business for yourself, but not by yourself."

By contrast, retailing, which involves staying in one place and hoping your customers will come to you, is relatively new. As a concept, retailing is under siege. Department stores and major retailers are finding it increasingly difficult to survive in a changing world. I am constantly amazed at the headstands and backflips the shopping malls are performing to attract and maintain retail traffic. Some malls have evolved into a series of entertainment centers, others have virtually become theme parks, complete with enormous tracts of land for car parking.

The retailer picks up the tab for trying to run a business in this environment, with high rents, restrictive contracts, and a lineup of competitors in close proximity.

No wonder everywhere you go you're faced with empty storefronts, going-out-of-business sales, and "For Lease" signs.

Compare this to the environment offered to customers who buy direct, enjoying personal, face-to-face, in-home service that includes delivery right to their door.

These customers have no parking hassles, don't suffer trailing tired kids through a shopping mall, and aren't rushing around, squeezing shopping between work and other commitments.

Cleaning products, clothing, cookware, cosmetics, giftware, home appliances, home decorating accessories, life insurance, jewelry, nutritional supplements, and telephone and Internet services are popular choices for people buying directly from others on a one-on-one basis.

How It Works

Most direct-selling companies have expanded their marketing system to include an additional and significant point of difference to the simple act of face-to-face direct selling. This is where the industry picks up its network marketing, or direct marketing, name and where it offers the opportunity to earn an outstanding income.

In network marketing, as an independent salesperson (known in the industry as a distributor or independent business owner), you are encouraged by your company to recruit others and earn commissions or bonuses on their sales, in addition to your own.

You build a team of independent salespeople, known as your *downline*.

Imagine being able to develop and manage your own business, without the traditional overhead, administrative nightmares, and constraints. If you're already in network marketing, you'll know your income isn't being eaten up by rent, staffing, inventory, and other costs associated with a retail business.

With a franchise, you would also be working to make an income for the franchiser and to pay your franchise fee. While network marketing carries one of the major benefits of a franchise, i.e., a clear, proven model on which to base your business, it can be operated with minimal start-up capital and relatively small ongoing overhead.

The real magic of network marketing comes when you have people in your downline who are also building a downline team of people who are also building a downline team of people who are also building a downline team . . .

People who are downline from you are not only working for themselves, but are also contributing to your income.

This building of a downline is known as duplication and it is here that the multilevel aspect comes in.

In the industry, duplication is sometimes described as the magic factor of five.

Put simply (purely as an example to illustrate how it works), you recruit five productive people who each recruit five productive people, and so on, five levels deep.

You work closely with your five people (you become their *upline*), training each of them to build their own strong downline. In turn, they keep duplicating in the same manner. Potentially you can have a team of thousands of people in your downline. When pooled together, the small bonuses the company pays you on the sales of each of them will add up to a big monthly bonus check for you. It's that big monthly check, often in the tens of thousands of dollars, that drives the high achievers in this industry.

Looking ahead to the long-term future, a properly developed network marketing business can provide you with residual income from people you have recruited and trained, long after your direct involvement has finished. This continuing flow of residual income is a unique advantage of network marketing, unlike traditional wages that stop the day you stop working. Although you have to keep working and maintain a small level of involvement to receive ongoing payments, it is possible to virtually retire and yet still receive a good income from the business you have built up.

This Book Is about You

Although the principles and experiences I share with you apply to every aspect of direct selling, I have written this book primarily to help you succeed in network marketing. Rather than relying on luck or chance, you should learn the necessary skills to be an active part of your own successes.

This book will teach you the principles that will help you achieve what millions of people have already achieved—a successful career through applying the techniques and making them work. I have learned these principles in both the field and in the corporate head office, working firsthand with thousands of people in different countries, over 25 years. I have consulted with the management of a range of network marketing companies, who sell a wide diversity of products and services, and have found the principles apply universally. Follow them and you'll discover that you can enjoy a career with rewards exactly equal to how hard—and how smart—you work.

This book is about working with yourself and with other people. It's not about getting involved with pyramid schemes (which are illegal, as they should be). It's not about motivating you to approach and sponsor large numbers of total strangers, or encouraging you to pester friends and family to the extent that they cross the street to avoid you.

You'll learn how to build a solid network marketing business, without outlaying a large amount of money or carrying bulk quantities of product. A network marketing business that can be run from your own home, with unlimited potential, minimal overhead, positive tax advantages, and no bad debt risks.

This is a "How to Do It" book that will give you the guidelines to successfully grow your own network marketing business as a distributor or independent business owner—a business you can start even if you're already employed. It will show you not only how to survive but how to thrive and achieve a lifestyle you would hardly dare dream possible.

Many successful people in network marketing started part-time before they operated their business full-time. In fact, for most people, I recommend this as the best way to start. For women who have chosen to leave the workforce to raise a family, network marketing provides a perfect bridge back to a two-income family.

If you have a partner who is able and willing to support you financially as you develop your business, seize the moment. When you achieve success, both of you will enjoy the wonderful lifestyle network marketing offers.

Millions of women and men throughout the world have already found that network marketing is perfect for them. The future offers unheralded opportunities as network marketing fits in perfectly with the new way of doing things. Network marketing frees us from the constraints of corporate life and the restrictions of a retailer's ever lengthening opening hours. It allows us to do what matters—create a worthwhile income and still be able to spend time with our family and friends, doing the things we enjoy most.

The opportunities offered by network marketing are vibrant and expanding. The people who will thrive in network marketing over the years ahead are those who travel through life with an open mind, an ability to accept that things have changed and will keep changing. When confronted with these changes, keep your mind open to them. See prejudice for what it is—prejudging—mostly caused by ignorance or fear of the unknown. Prejudice against network marketing comes from those who feel threatened by it, those who have not taken the time to find out what it really is and those who doubt their own ability to succeed in a reward-for-results industry.

To my mind, you can't have more compelling evidence of the future success of network marketing than its adoption by the dynamic *Fortune* 500 companies. They have recognized the need to diversify away from traditional retail distribution channels to network marketing, a viable alternative that allows ordinary, everyday people (like the people who live next door to the people who live next door to you!) to benefit.

Examples of businesses that include network marketing as part of their overall marketing include Citigroup, the world's largest financial institution; Teleglobe, the world's largest telecom network; and Prodigy, one of the world's first full-service Internet service providers. AT&T, IBM, and GM are also successfully incorporating network marketing into their strategies.

Network marketing offers you independence and freedom. It provides the chance to own a low-overhead business for a small investment and share in wealth that truly reflects the work you put in and the results you achieve.

This book will help you achieve the results you want. Step by step it will show you what to focus on to unleash the million-dollar potential of network marketing. If you're looking for "the big idea," you won't find it in this book. There is no one easy answer. Success in network marketing, as in any business, comes from doing a number of things right. That's why this book is packed with countless little ideas, which, when used together, have been proven to be essential to build a million-dollar business.

This book is not filled with inspirational stories of other people's successes. You can hear those stories from your upline, firsthand from the podium at the next seminar you attend, or read about them in the numerous books and magazines that testify to the success enjoyed by other people in network marketing.

This is a book about you.

Just How Big Is Direct Selling?

An estimated 12 million people are involved in direct selling in North America and more than 30 million worldwide. Most are women (73 percent) although nearly a third are men or couples. Approximately 90 percent of all direct sellers spend less than 30 hours per week on their network marketing business, with more than 50 percent spending less than 10 hours.

Worldwide sales grew between 1990 and 2000 from approximately $34 billion to an estimated $100 billion, of which over $23 billion occurs in the United States.

The United States Direct Selling Association claims that "virtually every consumer product or service can be purchased through direct selling and more than 50 percent of the American public has purchased goods or services through direct selling." The range of products they buy is immense and includes automotive products, clothing, cosmetics and skincare, financial services, jewelry, herbal tonics, household products, Internet and phone services, nutritional and diet products, public utilities, travel, and water filtration.

These are approximate breakdowns of sales by product groupings as reported by the United States Direct Selling Association:

Beauty, grooming and personal care	31%
Nutrition and wellness products	24%
Household cleaning products	12%
Services	7%
Home decorating accessories	5%
Housewares	4%
Other	17%

According to USDSA figures, the comparison between multilevel and single-level direct selling companies in their organization is as follows:

	Multilevel	Single-level
Number of firms	80.4%	19.6%
Sales dollars	73.5%	26.5%
Number of sales people	81.7%	18.3%

One-on-one selling is the primary method used to sell a product or service. Sales strategies, as reported in the DSA's salesforce survey, are as follows:

One-on-one	72%
Party Plan	26%
Other	2%

CHAPTER 2

Are You Right for Network Marketing?

You think network marketing might be right for you. Maybe there's only a tiny flicker of interest. Or perhaps, a burning desire to give it a go. But, are you right for network marketing?

The first thing to know is, network marketing works.

Sure, sometimes it is hyped up by its overenthusiastic proponents. But it does work—if you do.

That's right. It works if you do.

Where Do You Want to Be?

Before you read further, take a few minutes to think about where you want your life to be in five years time.

Close your eyes and visualize your life . . . the house you will be living in, the lifestyle you and your family will be enjoying, the vacations you will be taking, the car you will be driving, your children's education . . .

Picture every detail . . . the colors, the textures, the sights, sounds, and smells.

Now, open your eyes, take a few deep breaths and . . . double your income. Close your eyes once more and go through the pictures in your mind again, visualizing the lifestyle you will enjoy now that you are earning twice as much as before.

Now make the sky the limit and picture it again with five times your current income.

Finally, tell yourself that no matter how amazing the lifestyle you have just visualized, you can achieve it, just as countless others have. You can tell yourself that with confidence. Because it's true.

If you are prepared to work, nothing compares with network marketing in its ability to deliver the income you'll require for the lifestyle you dream of. Network marketing allows you to run your own business, without having to find and risk a large up-front investment. And best of all, you can achieve it while enjoying the flexibility and freedom of spending more time living your life the way you want to.

How else can you start a business that offers so much potential for so little up-front cost? However, there are no guarantees. As I said earlier—and you'll hear and use this phrase yourself many times throughout your network marketing career—it works if you do.

Network marketing is not, never has been, and never will be an easy route to riches, so beware those who oversell you on the opportunity. As with everything else in life, part-time effort will not yield full-time results. It takes consistent time, effort, and energy to build a network marketing business.

Who Are Network Marketers?

The world is full of countless network marketing success stories of $100,000-plus income earners who drive a company car, travel widely, and enjoy all the experiences, fun, and responsibilities that go with being at the helm of their own ship. It is also full of countless stories of people who are using their network marketing career to supplement the family income, provide quality education for their children, and afford luxuries like family holidays and new cars. These people are also enjoying amazing growth in their self-confidence and personal development, while meeting other interesting people and making lots of new friends. And, of course, there are countless people who have become millionaires, using the principles outlined in this book.

People with network marketing businesses come from all walks of life. They're from city and rural areas. They're married, divorced, and single. Some have families, some don't. Some are young, while others start in their so-called retirement years. There's no single profile of a successful person in network marketing other than a commitment to understand and apply the principles that lead to success.

Although they are selling an immensely diverse range of products, two things unite the most successful network marketers.

First, they believe in their product. Without a good product you cannot sustain long-term sales.

Second, they believe in duplication. Because, no matter how enthusiastic your commitment to the ethic of working hard, even if you work 50 or more hours a week, there is ultimately a limit to how much you can do.

Take, for example, a successful dentist. He can only fit in a certain number of appointments per week. When his appointment book is full, how can he increase his income? Only by increasing his fees until his patients start to feel the pain in their wallets more than in their teeth.

By contrast, when you're in network marketing, you have an unlimited number of opportunities to duplicate yourself and receive a share of the income from the people you bring into your business.

Duplicating Yourself

Duplication is not limited to your neighborhood, your city, or even your country. Many of the multimillionaires in the network marketing industry are people who started just like you and have developed businesses across the country and around the world.

The wisdom of having other people help you earn your income is well summarized in a comment J. Paul Getty is reported to have made: "I would rather have one percent of the efforts of one hundred people than 100 percent of my own efforts."

When you work for a salary or wages, you are being paid for your time, talent, and experience. The system is such that even the most talented, hard-working employee in a company is working to support other less productive employees and to produce profits for the owners. Compared with traditional employees, network marketers build businesses that produce incomes well beyond their own direct efforts.

No business that I know of more directly rewards results.

With all businesses, there is much to learn from the experiences of others. If you are prepared to do what it takes to succeed and to follow the steps outlined in this book, you will enjoy a successful network marketing career.

Empowering Women

Network marketing has empowered many millions of people to succeed in the world of business. Without prior training and with minimal capital investment, network marketing allows you to go straight to the top of your own business. And when you're at the top you can achieve your full potential without being subjected to someone else's commands.

Women, especially, are empowered by network marketing, which may be why they outnumber men by more than two to one in this industry.

Despite the great leap forward made by the women's movement late in the 20th century, the reality is that today there are still comparatively small numbers of women in the top corporate echelons. Sure, a few make the headlines, but most women are a long way from achieving equality of opportunity and salary—except in network marketing. For example, fewer than 5 percent of the *Fortune* 500 companies have women among their highest-paid executives.

If you are a woman, network marketing can give you freedom. The freedom to:

- Balance business and family ambitions.
- Use your natural talents and contribute to the family income.
- Develop a career without making unacceptable sacrifices.
- Choose your own income, without constraints.
- Run your own business your own way in your own hours.
- Slow down or stop for a period of time and start again, such as during and after pregnancy.
- Start part-time and develop into full-time, at your own pace.
- Adapt your level of involvement as you move into enjoying a happy retirement, running your business on a less than full-time basis and still enjoying residual income.

Network marketing will change your life. Your self-image, self-confidence, and self-reliance will all improve beyond your imagination. The dream can come true for you, when you start working the magic of network marketing.

CHAPTER 3

Where Do You Begin?

The first commandment of network marketing is *Sell product*. The second commandment is *Duplicate*.

Follow both commandments equally and you will achieve the success you desire.

Your income will be directly related to the amount of product you and your downline sell. Stay clear of any network marketing company that tells you otherwise. The size of every check you receive will depend on the volume of orders produced by you and the people you recruit.

When starting your network marketing business there are three key elements to evaluate: the products, the plan, and the company.

The Products

Begin by choosing products to which you're attracted, products you can get passionate about, products you'll be able to excite others about.

Look for quality products that are unique or have unique elements to them.

Look for "the big idea," the reason why the products exist that you can easily talk about with your customers and prospects. Ask yourself: Does the product have any magic in it? For example, Nutrimetics, a network marketing skincare and cosmetics company, pioneered natural skincare, not just among network marketing companies but among all skincare companies. This will always be its magic factor.

While there are many successful network marketing companies selling durable products, my advice is to seriously consider products that are consumable, because repeat orders are the fuel of our business. If you choose durable products, check that the company regularly releases new products (which will give you repeat business from your client base). Check also that the cost of demonstration products is not going to be prohibitive; it could discourage people from joining you in your business.

Let's look at the difference between consumable and durable products. Imagine you're selling vitamins. Your new customer buys a month's supply from you. The product works well (because you've elected to join a reputable company with excellent products). From that one original sale, followed by regular servicing, you can develop a customer for life, as she will regularly replace the product each time it is used up. Compare that scenario with, say, selling a set of high-quality saucepans. There's every chance you won't sell that customer a replacement saucepan for another 20 years.

Candles, cleaners and other household items, cosmetics, food, hair care, nutritional supplements, vitamins, and weight loss products are all good network marketing products because they are consumed and repurchased on a regular basis.

Another consideration is that lower-priced consumable products make it financially easier for you to start your own business and to attract others to join you.

Long-distance calling, Internet access, and utilities are also perfect for network marketing, as they are not only consumed, they have the additional advantage of requiring no inventory or delivery.

The Remuneration Plan

Make sure the remuneration plan is one that suits your needs.

The plan is the basis on which your income will flow. Study the plan carefully until you fully understand it. When you are recruiting and sponsoring you will want to explain the plan to prospects and get them excited about it too.

Is the plan simple? The less complicated it is, the easier it will be for you and the people you recruit to understand and explain to others. Successful network marketing businesses grow when everything you do is simple and duplicable.

Does the plan pay your commission on the price you buy for, or the price you sell for? There is a significant difference. For example, if the commission rate sounds attractive at 40 percent, it might not be quite so attractive if it's 40 percent of the wholesale rate, compared with, say, 25 percent of the retail rate. If the retail price is double the wholesale price, then the 40 percent is effectively halved to only 20 percent of the selling price.

When I first started selling for a network marketing company I remember the buzz of driving home from my first show, doing the math in my head and thinking, "Wow, I sold $500 worth tonight, so 40 percent of that is $200." Imagine my disappointment at the end of the month, when my commission check was less than I anticipated. When we sell $500, we tend to think $500, not the wholesale price. So make sure you understand very clearly what your commission is based on.

Look at how much the plan pays out at the level you intend working your business. If you intend working part-time, ask yourself if the commissions are high enough to provide you, and the people you recruit, with an attractive income. Nothing motivates a person to leave network marketing faster than not making enough money in the first few months as they build their business.

Some plans require you to reach high levels before the income becomes attractive. This can discourage a potentially good person from sticking with the opportunity long enough to see the potential develop.

Other plans require a high level of personal activity before you can earn significant dollars from your downline. Find out whether there are limitations on the number of people you can personally sponsor, or how much *width* (personal sponsoring) you must achieve before taking advantage of the *depth* in your organization (people who have been sponsored by others in your downline).

Some plans work on a points system, and it takes time to learn and understand them. Make sure you fully understand each different plan, so when you select a company you're comparing "apples with apples."

As you learn how the company will pay your commissions and bonuses you may encounter a world of new phrases, such as: average order, BP (bonus points), BV (bonus volume), generational bonus, infinity bonus program, leadership bonus, overrides, PV (personal volume), seminar qualification, training bonus, sales volume. The remuneration plan itself takes on different names—compensation plan, commission plan, business plan, marketing plan, and others. This unique network marketing language can be bewildering to a newcomer.

Keep asking questions about any areas you're unsure of until you have a clear picture of how the plan works. Ask for examples. Ask also how the company recognizes successes. This will be important for you as you build and motivate your own downline. If the company has a culture of recognition, as most network marketing companies do, this will help your success.

The Company

Will you like working with the company and its people? If the company has its own culture, its own magic, you could find this generates an energy that you will radiate as you build your business. Does the company have experienced and charismatic leadership? Is the staff enthusiastic, professional, and friendly?

Check that the company is run efficiently. Is it easy to place orders? How long does it take to deliver your order? Does the company have a problem with backorders? How quickly will you be paid? How are problems resolved?

Is the company operating with an e-business mindset? Does it support its distributors with an up-to-date, attractive Web site that you can link into and online purchasing and sales systems? Does it allow you to easily track your business from your home PC? Does it have information hotlines and tele- or video-conferencing facilities? Will the Web site appeal to potential recruits?

The more backup support provided, the less time you will spend running the business and the more time you will have available to spend on building it.

Most of all, ask yourself: Are you sure this is a company you will be proud to represent?

You may want to join a company that is just starting up. Provided the company and its products are plausible you could get caught up in the excitement of being in on the ground floor.

Alternatively, you may wish to join a well-established company and benefit from the experience and reputation the company has gained.

Either way, the day you start in the business you are starting your own ground-floor opportunity. Whether you join one of the big ones or a newcomer, it's never too late. The sooner you start, the sooner you can grow. Your ground-floor opportunity is there because you will be bringing the product and the opportunity to your customers and potential recruits for the first time.

If a company is well established and appears to be reputable, yet you have never heard of it, don't be too concerned. Most major marketing companies traditionally spend millions of dollars in the media promoting their brand name and driving the market to the retailers. By contrast, network marketing companies rely on word of mouth advertising, a much stronger and more convincing one-on-one way of building their brand.

Don't be put off if you don't see the company advertising in magazines or on television. Most network marketing companies' products compete successfully against major international brands in the face of extensive and expensive brand advertising campaigns.

Network marketing is another way (many say a better way) of doing things. It works in the face of competition from some of the biggest-spending image-building companies in the world. Amway, Enrich, Excel, Herbalife, Mannatech, Mary Kay, New Image, Nu Skin, Reliv, Shaklee, Tupperware, Usana, and Watkins are among the many network marketing companies who each enjoy an impressive market share in very competitive retail fields.

Direct selling giant Avon is an excellent example of the power of person-to-person selling over retail.

Instead of expensive media advertising, network marketing companies use their marketing budgets to pay distributors' commissions and bonuses, to run distributors' promotions, to arrange distributors' training, to hold international seminars and to buy company cars for their successful distributors. The marketing budget is not given to the major television companies and the publishers of glossy magazines. It's spent on you!

I recommend joining a company that is a member of the Direct Selling Association (DSA) or the Multi-Level Marketing International Association (MLMIA). DSA members adhere to strict integrity criteria in both their products and the way they conduct their business. A complete and up-to-date list of DSA organizations and their addresses is available on the Internet through the World Federation Of Direct Selling Associations at *www.dsa.org*. Look for the World Federation of Direct Selling Associations (WFDSA) link. This will take you to the WFDSA site.

Here you'll find "DSA List by Country," which you can click into, for your local national DSA address. Your local office of the Direct Selling Association will be happy to give you a current list of their member companies and answer any questions you may have.

You'll find you can link from the *www.dsa.org* Web site to each member company's own Web site, a quick and easy way for you to visit each company. Look for the "About Our Member Companies" link.

U.S. member companies and key international DSA addresses are included in appendices at the end of this book.

Obviously, to join more than one company would be unwise, as you will need to keep your focus in one direction to succeed to your full potential. Clear direction and focused activity are fundamental to your success.

Once chosen, the company will welcome you with open arms. They will become your business partner and handle all the back-end work, leaving you free to focus on building your own business and making money.

Be Your Best Customer

Finding your first customer is simple. Every successful network marketer started with this one. It's you!

Be your first customer and your best customer.

Love your product. Use it always. Everywhere. Keep discovering great things about it and new ways to use it. Take every opportunity to include your products as gifts. For birthdays and Christmas. Mother's Day and Father's Day. Thank-you gifts. Hostess gifts. And gifts for any other occasion you can think of.

As a distributor you'll be able to buy products inexpensively. More important, your absolute knowledge of, belief in, enthusiasm for, and commitment to your products will rub off onto your customers. It will also set the standard for the downline organization you are building.

Enthusiasm is contagious. As your firsthand knowledge of your product grows, so will your confidence and enthusiasm when selling to others. Nothing beats personal experience and the endorsement that comes from always using the product yourself. Also, imagine your lack of credibility if a guest in your home caught you using a competitor's product!

When you're using your products day in, day out, you will discover the real benefits of using them. You'll find you won't be able to stop yourself telling other people about these benefits.

Develop your own story. Instead of a bland, "It's a great product," build a testimonial based on your own experience. Use the product for one week, then one month, and note what happens. Your presentation becomes more believable when you have personal conviction. This will only come from using the products and experiencing the results for yourself. Become a living testimony for your products and share your enthusiasm with everyone you meet!

One of my best-ever personal endorsements for a skincare product came from an unlikely source, my son David.

A few years ago, my then teenage son spent a long time in the bathroom preparing for a date. Teenage boys, as we know, are not famous for their personal grooming habits. If bathroom time was any indicator, this date was very special.

Finally he emerged, crestfallen. As part of making everything perfect he had shaved so thoroughly he raised a red rash on his face.

The company I worked for had just released a product designed to purify, calm, and settle the skin (a woman's skin, not a teenage boy's). I saturated a tissue with the product and held it to his face. Within minutes, his skin had settled and all was well again.

The first time I told this story, I saw immediate interest. So I kept telling the story, and my ability to promote our new product never looked back . . . only because I was using the products, experimenting with them, discovering what they could do.

If you are selling jewelry or fashion, wear it—always. If you're selling candles, display them throughout your home. If you're selling vitamins, line your bathroom shelves with them and take them regularly. Use your cooking utensils in your kitchen so you can appreciate their superior performance firsthand. Use only your company's skincare and cosmetics on your skin.

Your experience with your products will provide you with powerful personal endorsements. For example:

- "I had such dry skin before I started using this moisturizing cream."
- "I have lost weight before, but never managed to keep it off as easily as I can now."
- "We've cut the grocery bill for our family by $20 every week."
- "Our telephone bill is at least $20 less than it was before we signed up and yet we're making more long-distance calls."

Customers will always respond more readily to a story than they will to information about the products you are promoting.

The only thing more contagious than enthusiasm is the lack of it. You can't expect your customers to embrace your products unless they can sense your unrelenting enthusiasm for, loyalty to, and love of them.

When you are your own best customer, you become a walking, talking advertisement for your product.

So, select your product, your plan, and your company with care, and then begin your journey to making your first million!

CHAPTER 4

Why Do I Love Network Marketing?

W hy do I love network marketing? Let me count the ways! Understanding network marketing means letting go of your current way of thinking. Network marketing is a different way of doing things and of achieving sensationally different results.

Here are my top ten reasons why I know you will find network marketing, and the opportunities it offers, so exciting.

Ownership

There are few comparable opportunities to own your own business for such a small initial investment. And there is nothing more empowering than being in control of your business and your life.

Support

Although you own your own business, you're not alone. You become part of a team (your upline) and you build a team (your downline). The network marketing company you have chosen to join will be committed to supporting you. You will be amazed at the generosity shown to you by others in the business. You will find a willingness to help, guide, and support you that you won't find in any other industry. Network marketing engenders a unique spirit of sharing.

Training

You don't need a sales or business background or prior experience with the product you're selling. Your upline and your network marketing company will help you learn the necessary skills. Every network marketing company provides training materials and runs training sessions, seminars, and conferences to help their distributors. If you have committed people in your upline, they will mentor you as you grow, just as you will do later for the people you recruit.

There are numerous network marketing books, magazines, and audio- and videotapes available to help you gain knowledge and learn new techniques. Provided you have the desire and you're prepared to do what it takes, you'll quickly learn the skills required for success.

Versatility

Network marketing suits people of all ages, although most companies won't start anyone younger than 18 without a parent's signature. I know of people who started while at college and others in their 80s who are still earning income from their network marketing business.

People have found success in network marketing after coming from highflying corporate positions, professional careers, and trade occupations. Network marketing millionaires may have been housewives, shop assistants, teachers, nurses, social workers, or unemployed, proving that this business suits anyone who is prepared to work for results.

Part-Time or Full-Time

You can test the waters by starting your business in your spare time, while still working for your existing employer, and develop it into your full-time career whenever you want. In North America over 9 million people work their network marketing business part-time, topping up the family income and enhancing the family's lifestyle.

A key advantage of network marketing is that you can proceed at your own pace. Many times I have seen a part-time dabbler go on to become a top income earner and move into network marketing full-time. Similarly, I have seen many partners join the business once it has been established, allowing the couple to work together and enjoy sharing the network marketing lifestyle.

Low Overhead

There are few overhead costs, although these grow as your business develops. You'll have expenses for your vehicle, telephone, literature, office supplies, printing, postage, and, probably, a professional to help prepare your personal annual tax returns (a deductible cost that can more than pay itself, as you enjoy the available tax advantages). Most network marketing people work from home. There are no office rental costs, and some of your existing household expenses may be tax deductible. Many network marketing companies provide a company car once your business reaches a certain level—a big bonus! Plus, you're given opportunities to travel internationally to seminars in exotic locations at the company's expense. If you're selling a physical product (i.e., not telecommunications, services, or utilities), your costs will include demonstration materials, product samples, and gifts (purchased at a big discount). Compare these overheads with the cost of running a traditional business.

Flexibility

You work with the people you choose to work with, and you work the hours you choose to work. Unlike many corporate careers, the harder you work in network marketing the bigger your paycheck. You're not working to make your boss look good, you're working for yourself. Network marketing gives you the flexibility to spend more time with your family, even involving them in the business in small ways. You can work around school hours and other family commitments and take your vacation when it suits you, not your manager or the HR department. You can participate in your favorite sporting and leisure activities without feeling guilty and enjoy them at off-peak times without the crowds.

Personal Growth

Network marketing is a fast track to personal growth. Your growth in self-confidence, communication, and leadership skills never stops. You'll have access to courses and seminars that will include training and development in leadership, motivation, sales skills, personal growth, business management, and communications. You'll learn while you earn and develop invaluable skills that will benefit you in other aspects of your life. And you'll be stimulated by working around people who are positive, enthusiastic, creative, and successful.

Unlimited Potential

With network marketing you have the potential to make anything from a little extra spending money to an outstanding income. Your earning potential is not limited by hours in the day. Network marketing offers you the reverse of the normal corporate structure, where you can spend a lifetime waiting for the people above you to be promoted, move on, or retire before you can move up the ladder. In the corporate world it's difficult to achieve the quantum leaps in income that network marketing can provide. And with network marketing you will find people will want to help you succeed, because they know your success contributes to their success.

Fulfillment

Making new friends, socializing, and being part of the success of others is a great part of network marketing. Imagine the thrill of boarding a plane headed for a seminar in an exotic location, traveling with the people you recruited, motivated, trained, and supported toward that achievement. Helping others achieve their potential is immensely rewarding.

You will also find fulfillment in working for a company with integrity. Every network marketing company that belongs to the Direct Selling Association pledges to offer a minimum 30-day guarantee on their products, so there's no risk to you if a customer cancels an order or returns product. You can make your sales freely, relaxed in the knowledge that you have sound financial and ethical backing.

You can see why I love network marketing and what it offers. But a word of caution. There is no easy way to success. There are no corners to cut. If you are prepared to pay the price of hard work and perseverance, you can find unlimited success in network marketing. It's a vibrant, exciting, magical industry. Network marketing is a people business, a growth business that fits perfectly with the dot-com revolution that is sweeping the world. Network marketing is a business with unlimited opportunities for growth and for you to grow with it.

PART TWO

Selling

Your Way to

Success

CHAPTER 5

But I Can't Sell . . .

If you've never sold before, you could be thinking to yourself "But I can't sell." Yet, you can sell. You have already mastered your first step, by selling yourself on your product. Now, build from that positive start.

Knowledge = confidence = sales. You'll find that the more you learn, the more you earn!

There are hundreds of excellent books, audiotapes, and videotapes on selling that can help you increase your selling skills. Talk with your upline about what they recommend and what the company has available as training tools. Subscribe to industry magazines. Popular titles include *Upline, Network Marketing Lifestyles, MLM Insider, Success*, and *Opportunity*.

Get to Know the Customer

The first lesson you'll learn is that selling is not about you, it's about the person you're selling to.

We are all self-centered. If you're not sure about this, think what happens when you're shown a group photo. Your most natural response is immediately to scan the photo to find yourself. "How do I look?" you wonder. Only after finding yourself do you start to look at the others in the picture.

Always remember that most people are concerned more about themselves than anyone else. It follows, therefore, that people will like you when you demonstrate that you are interested in them. And people buy from people they like. If they don't like you in the first place, they certainly won't like what you're selling. The more time you spend getting to know your customers, the better foundation you build for your future relationship.

Don't skimp on this step. Sometimes we feel uncomfortable, wondering that if we ask too much the other person will think we are prying. Don't believe it. Start asking questions and you will soon find the other person warming to you and opening up. People are interested in themselves and in people who are interested in them, so take your time getting to know people before you start introducing your products.

While you are getting to know your customers, you are building an invaluable profile of them, one of the greatest business tools of all. Not only are you able to offer the right product and service now, but in the future too, as your company releases new products.

Service: Your Competitive Edge

Today, as consumers, we have higher expectations of service. We're more value conscious, more knowledgeable, and less trusting. This is where network marketing gives you a competitive edge over other ways your customer might buy the product. The days of the small Mom-and-Pop style of retailer are numbered, giving way to the big chains who present their products in what is really nothing more than a swept-up warehouse. Trying to get personal service in a big store is now one of life's major challenges. Large retailers rely on merchandising to sell the products, counting on store layout, advertising, and pack designs to make the sale. They offer a massive selection but few staff to serve and guide customers to the best product for them.

By contrast, in network marketing you have the ability to understand your customers and their concerns, then specifically pinpoint solutions. This will always give you your competitive edge.

The Magical Selling Triangle

There's another way to look at what makes a successful salesperson. It's what I call the Magical Selling Triangle. The following illustration depicts a typical selling scenario.

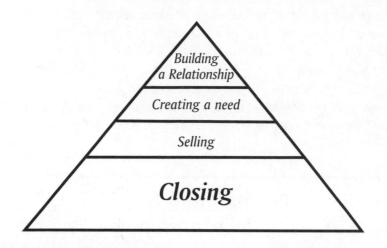

BUILDING A RELATIONSHIP

Most salespeople know they have to spend time getting to know the customer. A few hasty questions are asked, to get that over and done with. Then it's down to business.

CREATING A NEED

Next they move on to convincing their customer they need the product. A little more time is spent on this step.

SELLING

Now they're really getting into it. They're salespeople, so they had better start selling! They know the product inside out—prices, ingredients, and numerous features. They're thinking, "If I keep talking, I'll overcome any objections before they have time to think about them." A large part of the presentation is taken up with this stage.

CLOSING

Finally, they've covered everything they can think of, so they start working hard at closing the sale, thinking that otherwise all their efforts will be wasted. This is where they turn on the persuasion, the charm, and the pressure. The bulk of time is spent on this step.

Sounds like a nightmare, doesn't it? As customers, we've all been in situations like this. I bet you, like I, didn't buy the product, or if you did it was a one-time sale and you'll keep a safe distance from the salesperson in the future. No one likes to be "sold." We all like to make the decision to buy, because the product feels right for us.

Now let's do the trick of turning the triangle upside down and making a few changes to it, to reveal the magic selling power of a successful salesperson.

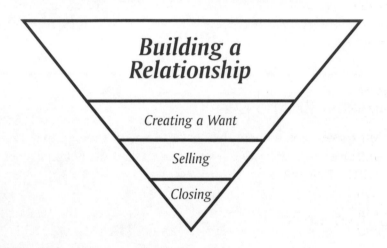

BUILDING A RELATIONSHIP

It takes time to develop a relationship, so spend most of your effort getting to know your customer. Discover what they are about. Show them that you are interested in them and understand them, as you locate their hot buttons.

This is the time, if you're listening hard enough, when you'll hear your customer telling you how they will benefit from using your product.

CREATING A WANT

We make most of our decisions emotionally and then justify the decision with logic. For example, "I want that new dress, and it will be perfect if I am invited somewhere special." If you doubt what I'm saying, think about how you made one of your most life-changing decisions, choosing your partner. Was it made emotionally or logically? Even our most important decisions are based on emotion, not logic, so focusing on what people want rather than what you think they need is the key to success in selling.

SELLING

Based on what you know about your customer and how your products will benefit them, you can concentrate on selecting the product, program, color choice, size, or option that best suits them. Objections can be raised and answered in an environment of mutual trust, respect, and interest.

CLOSING

At this stage you can move quickly to the close, confirming and writing up the order. The customer has made up their mind already and doesn't need to be sold.

Which way up is your selling triangle? Compare the original and the new one. You'll see that successful selling is much less about you and your product line, and much more about your customer and their life.

The Difference Between the "Need" and the "Want"

People buy what they want to buy, rather than what they need. We all *need* to eat healthier food and yet we *want* the ease, convenience, and taste of take-out food, which is why that industry is booming.

I recall, as a teenager, deciding it was time to buy my first lipstick. I walked up to the beauty counter at a major department store and asked for the bright pink lipstick I wanted. The sales consultant looked at my (admittedly spotty) skin and decided, quite correctly, that I "needed" skin care. I waited patiently as she recommended a comprehensive skincare regimen, then found an excuse to walk out. She didn't get the sale, but the store on the next block did, where I bought the lipstick I wanted. The customer knows best!

CHAPTER 6

The Seven Deadly Sins of Selling

It's easy to make mistakes on your way to learning how to be a great sales person. These mistakes are what I call my Seven Deadly Sins of Selling. I'll start with the most dangerous first.

The First Deadly Sin of Selling: Talking Too Much

Yes! Talking too much is the biggest mistake you can make, because when you're talking, you're not listening. And when you're not listening, you're not learning about your customer's ambitions, desires, feelings, lifestyle, needs, preferences, thoughts, and wants. When you come to make the sale, you'll probably miss your target.

Unfortunately, "talking" people are attracted to selling, hence the frequently painted portrait of the salesperson as a smooth talker.

Talking too much is sometimes a sign of nervousness, as the salesperson turns on a torrent of words to overcome his or her anxiety. If this sounds like you, unlearn the talking habit and learn the listening one.

The quickest route to building great relationships with your customers is to let them do the talking. Your job is to ask the right questions, listen to the answers, and learn from them.

When you listen carefully to your customers they will tell you how to sell to them.

What sort of questions will you ask? Try these "getting-to-know-you" questions:

- Where do you live?
- Have you lived there long?
- How do you like living there?
- Where do you work?
- Do you enjoy what you do?
- What work does your partner do?
- Do you have a family?
- How old are your children?
- What school do your children attend?
- Are you a busy person?
- What do you do in your spare time?

Or try these "getting-to-know-the-product" questions:

- Are you familiar with our product?
- Have you used our product before?
- What product are you currently using?
- What do you look for in this kind of product?
- What was the best one you used?
- Which one did you like least?
- Do you prefer products that are . . . (fill in your product's appropriate selling point, e.g., free of additives, original designs, locally made, etc.)?
- Do you have any specific problems . . . (again, linked to your product—skin sensitivities, food allergies, stress, weight gain, making ends meet, etc.)?
- Do you take vitamin supplements?
- Are you happy with your current weight?
- Are you totally happy with your diet?
- If you could change one thing about your diet (or skin or wardrobe . . .), what would it be?
- Do you smoke?
- Do you have any specific problems with your skin?
- When was the last time you had a color makeover?

You can ask questions to establish how comfortable your prospect is with purchasing direct:

- Where do you mostly shop?
- Do you buy any products direct?
- What products do you buy through mail order?
- Have you ever bought or tried to buy anything on the Internet?
- Would home delivery make your life easier?

Of course you can't and won't ask all of these. It's not *Twenty Questions.* Nor will every question suit every occasion. These are just idea starters. You know how to develop a conversation from there; you've been doing it every day of your life since you learned to talk! The aim is to find out as much as possible about your customer. Develop your own questions as openers that can lead into a product sale or recruiting interview.

The harder you listen to the response to the first question, the more appropriate your next question will be. If you're busy talking, or thinking about what you are going to say next, you won't enable your customer to develop a reasonable conversation. The more carefully you listen to and think about what's being said in the responses to your questions, the better position you will be in to introduce the pertinent benefits of your product or opportunity. Which brings us to the next deadly sin.

The Second Deadly Sin of Selling: Putting Product First

Don't put your product ahead of people. It's an easy trap to fall into, spending more time on your product or opportunity than on your customer. Only when you really know your customers can you honestly explain how your product will enhance their lives. It's your job as a salesperson to identify what your customer is looking for and then supply what is needed. This is why I encourage you to become your own best customer and learn what the product does, firsthand. Not how or why, but what it does for you, and will do for your customers. The benefit of it. Work with your upline or your company to determine how to best describe the ways your product will enhance your customers' lives.

Think about what people want in life. Most of us would own up to wanting at least half of the things on this contemporary-living wish list.

- To be healthier
- To be fitter
- To have more fun
- To have more time
- To look a little younger
- To look a little more attractive
- To look a little slimmer
- To save money

It's just the same for the business opportunity you offer with network marketing. Most people are looking for:

- More freedom
- More money
- More spare time
- More control over their lives
- More security
- More choices

How does your product or opportunity deliver what people are looking for? If you can succinctly answer that question, you have a good chance of making the sale.

The Third Deadly Sin of Selling: Focusing on Features, Not Benefits

It's all too easy to get excited about the features of your product or opportunity. The features are unimportant, apart from the benefits they produce.

When someone buys aspirin, it's because they want fast relief from a headache. Headache relief is the benefit of the aspirin. The aspirin's features and chemical ingredients are unimportant. The benefit that's wanted is headache relief.

It follows that if you want to sell aspirin, give someone a headache! In other words, whatever your product or opportunity, create a compelling reason for your customer to buy it. Think, "What's in it for me?" from your customer's perspective.

Too often, we make the mistake of focusing on how good the product or opportunity is, rather than how it will make life better for the customer.

If you're selling, say, an energy drink, you won't need to know by rote the table of ingredients—vitamins, minerals, trace elements, or whatever. The thing that is most significant is the difference the drink makes to your well-being. That's the difference you can honestly and enthusiastically tell your customer about. How your increased energy, vitality, and stamina help you cope with the stresses of the day. Don't fall into the trap of thinking you are required to be a walking encyclopedia, crammed with details about every aspect of your products.

Whatever you're selling, it's always the benefit that counts. But always be ready to answer questions raised by your customers by learning as much as you can about your product.

When you're sitting face-to-face with your customer, you're not alone. If you get a question you can't answer, say so, and then make a note of the question. Ask your upline, your sponsor, or the company, then come back to your customer when you have found the answer.

Resist the temptation to slip into a high-powered selling mode because you think that's what salespeople do. Just as you wouldn't when you're telling your friends about a good television program, movie, or restaurant, you shouldn't when you're telling them about your great products.

The Fourth Deadly Sin of Selling: Taking a "One-Size-Fits-All" Approach

Treating all your customers the same way will reduce your chances of success. Just as we all look, speak, and act differently, we all think differently. Some people are 100 percent analytical. For them, logical considerations like price, size, and value are prime concerns. At the other extreme, some people are totally emotional and will respond best to ideas, anecdotes, and other people's experiences with the products. Give them too much detail and you'll notice they become impatient and lose interest.

Hone your listening skills to help you determine the makeup of each of your customers so you can adapt your presentation to suit. Your success rate will increase when people feel comfortable with you. If you are too overpowering or overwhelming, you will turn off many people. If you are "underwhelming," people may not respond to you, because you don't seem confident about what you are telling them. Try these simple techniques to increase your ability to adapt to different communication styles, build rapport, and make your customers feel at ease.

- Sit beside, not across from them.
- Match (some call it mirror) their body language, level of eye contact, and posture.
- Adjust the tone and pitch of your voice to your customer's.
- Learn to recognize and respond to the signals your customer is giving out so that you can complement their communication style.

Treat every customer as an individual and balance your presentation to include both logical and emotional information until you see which approach your customer responds to best. (You will find this subject covered more in Chapter 27 and there are many books available on this specialist subject.)

The Fifth Deadly Sin of Selling: Offering Too Much Choice

Today we are bombarded with choices. The result for most of us is confusion, frustration, and "switching off."

When we walk into a book, video, or music store, the range of choices offered can overwhelm us. How do we choose from all those options? If it's one of the smarter stores you'll probably see a sign saying "Staff Selections" or "Staff Favorites." You'll be interested because there's something especially appealing about the recommendation of a professional or someone in the know. Similarly, a display of the top ten sellers dramatically boosts sales, because for many buyers, there's security in popularity. We feel, "If so many people are buying this book or CD, then it must be good." And we all know that authors and performing artists depend on the best-seller list or the hit parade to make it big-time.

Similarly, in a good restaurant, a skilled waiter will specifically recommend one or two dishes to help you order well.

Use this technique when you're doing your presentation. Choose a group of products (maybe two to four) and during your presentation talk about these products as the "must haves." Support each product with a short and irresistible reason why you personally recommend it.

People buy with confidence when they know they're not taking a risk. Learn from the success of the top-ten and bestseller approach to promoting videos, music, and books and apply it to your product.

Part of the magic of network marketing is that each sale is to a customer you will continue to service. You can afford to take it gradually. There will be plenty of time in the future to sell more of your range to them. You're the expert, and they will be guided by your advice on the "must have" products. Start by keeping it simple, focusing on a few core products to avoid confusion.

For example, if you represented skincare products and wanted to sell a particularly soothing eye gel that helps protect the sensitive skin around the eye area from the damage emitted by a computer screen, here's how the conversation could go:

"Do you work at a computer for at least two hours most days?"

You immediately have your customer's attention, because you are talking quite specifically about them.

"How do your eyes feel after a few hours in front of the screen? Tired, dry, or strained? That's because the light emitted from computer screens can stress the fragile, sensitive skin around your eyes, not to mention the lines that will form from squinting at your screen hour after hour. That's why we formulated this soothing gel. It keeps your eyes feeling calm and refreshed and helps protect your skin from damage."

Who could put their hand up for using a computer then not put their hand up for the eye gel?

It's a quick and simple technique that works. If a customer asks how the product works, then you can talk about the formulation and the ingredients. But most customers don't want the formulation, they want the benefit—soothing relief from tired eyes and protection against potential aging.

You could use the same technique, for example, for aromatherapy oil burners. If you asked the question, "Do you feel washed-out at the end of the day?" you would probably get 100 percent agreement.

Now offer the solution.

"Late afternoon is when many of us feel our lowest. Our body clock tells us our energy reserves are all but used up. There's nothing worse than feeling too tired to do all the things you want to. We have the perfect solution. Burn this soothing aromatherapy oil next to you while you relax for a few minutes. Breathe in the soft, soothing fragrance. It's not at all overpowering and it will gently lift your spirits and revive your energy level. You'll actually enjoy your evenings again, instead of wasting them slumped in front of the television!"

Whatever your product range, whether it's a special pan to make cooking easier and healthier, an amazing utensil that reduces food preparation time, or a plastic container that keeps food fresher longer, keep your presentation simple, snappy, and to the point.

Bring the product to life with vivid word pictures, demonstrations, and powerful promises that will make your customers want it. Don't drown your customers in choice or in details.

The Sixth Deadly Sin of Selling: Not Responding to Objections

Too many salespeople gloss over objections, but in order to move on you have to accept or address the barrier that has been raised. Listen hard to what's being said, and what's not being said, to understand why an objection has arisen. Think of an objection as a request for more information.

Take time to think, then give a direct, open, and honest answer. Know that you're not going to win them all. The sale agreed to reluctantly or under duress has no future. Your business depends on future sales and building long-term relationships with people who respect you. They will recognize it if you try to squirm away from answering an objection. You want their trust and confidence. You want them to like you. So respect and respond to every objection with honesty and sincerity. When you realize the objections mean the customer does not wish to proceed, do not push.

The Seventh Deadly Sin of Selling: Forgetting to Close

I often see salespeople do everything right, then omit to ask for the order. Everything else is a waste of time unless you ask for the order. There comes a point in your presentation when it's time to close the sale.

How do you close and ask for the order?

Ask!

Don't be afraid to help your customer along. Say to them, "These are the colors I recommend for you," or "That bracelet looked stunning on you." If possible, reinforce your recommendation by handing the recommended products to your customer. If a customer order form is used, mark the products you recommend. A highlighter pen is quick and stands out more if you're working from a list of products.

There are many different ways you can ask for the sale, depending on the personality of your customers. They range from the gentle to the direct, and each works.

Often the most direct works best. Simply ask for the order. "Can I order that for you today?"

If your customer is hesitant by nature, using a deadline could stir them into a decision. "This offer is only available tonight (or until . . .)."

One good idea is to be gently positive and simply assume your customer is going to place an order. "All I need now is your address . . ."

Occasionally, "incentivizing" the sale by giving a gift or discount may work, but you won't make a million if you always give away your profit. However, if your company has a gift-with-purchase offer, use it to the fullest. "If you order today, I will include this gift."

Another way to bring your conversation to a positive close is to offer a choice. "Would you prefer the . . . (for example, Value or Deluxe) package?"

You will be amazed at how people respond to you when you close confidently. Experiment with each of those techniques to help you move the decision forward to a close. Use them all until you find which you're most confident with and which suit your different customers.

Once you have made your close, give your customers time and space to think and come to a decision. Don't talk again until they talk. Many positive decisions to buy have been made in the space of silence.

To build a successful business, there's also an "Eighth Deadly Sin of Selling" to avoid. It comes not during the selling process, but very soon after. I call it . . .

The Deadly Sin of Not Following Through

You cannot sustain a long-term business in sales without repeat customers. It's that simple.

All of us who have tried to master a sport, from golf to tennis or softball, know the second most important part is the follow-through. (The first is hitting the ball!)

In sports, the follow-through is the difference between hitting and hoping your ball is on course, and making sure it is.

In your business, follow-through is the difference between making a sale and making a customer.

The value of the commission on a sale is far greater when you view it over a longer time scale. Your investment in time spent getting to know your customer when making your first sale is paid back handsomely by the subsequent sales.

Follow every sale with a customer satisfaction call. Every time. No shortcuts. One action is better than one hundred good intentions. Just make the calls. Here's why:

- Follow-through is basic courtesy. You owe it to your customer to check on the performance of the products purchased from you.
- Follow-through gives you the opportunity to address any problems with the product. For example, correct application or correct usage. Perhaps there was an error with delivery. Every customer will appreciate the time you take to ensure all is well.
- Follow-through gives you the opportunity to keep your customer up-to-the-minute with new product releases and, over a period of time, gently extend the range of products being used.
- Follow-through establishes your credibility and develops your relationship, so your customer will feel comfortable calling you for advice or to reorder. This will help you to develop an ongoing reorder business.

- Follow-through enables you to ask for referrals from a satisfied customer.
- Follow-through builds your relationship with your customers, who then become your best prospects for building your downline business. It gives you an opening to introduce your customers to your business opportunity, as they start to appreciate how much you enjoy and benefit from being in network marketing.

From your first discussion with your customer, let them know that the special nature of your business and the service you give mean you will be keeping in touch with them regularly.

Ensure every customer has your name, address, and telephone details and knows you are happy to hear from them. When they do call, let them know their call is welcome.

Have small adhesive labels printed to place discretely on every product before delivery. "*To reorder, call Maxine, phone . . .*" Another idea is to have fridge magnets or telephone stickers printed with your name and contact details.

At least once a year:

- Thank your customers for their business, perhaps with a card, a handwritten note, or a small gift.
- Consider inviting your best customers to a customer appreciation party.

Despite all the offers placed in your customer's mailbox, all the mail-order catalogs, and all the publicity about selling through the Internet, no one will ever be able to match you in service. Your personality, your interest in your customer, and your follow-through will ensure you are famous for great customer service.

Work hard to avoid the "Seven Deadly Sins of Selling" and your sales will flourish. Avoid the "Eighth," and your business will flourish, too. Promise.

Too Much or Too Little?

Right now you could be thinking that it's all very well telling those with the "gift of the gab" to slow down, stop talking, and start listening, but what about me? My problem's just the opposite. I'm just not a gushing, selling kind of person.

My answer to this is simple. Virtually everything we do every day involves selling in one form or another. Success in this business is in telling, not selling. You don't "sell" your friend the idea of going to see a movie you know she will like. You tell her about it, because you know her, you know what her taste is and you know she will like the movie. You want her to enjoy the experience. With your natural enthusiasm, you're creating within her a desire to see it. She can't wait to get tickets. She's "sold" on it!

It's what you do daily in a dozen different ways. It's not just movies, it's television programs, books, and restaurants. And it's the same thing when we persuade our partner to take us out to dinner, or to get our children to clean their room. (I didn't say there was no challenge in it!)

If you can tell, you can sell. If you are sincere and genuinely interested in what you're selling, you'll find selling comes naturally. Of course, many network marketing companies are so proud of their products they claim they sell themselves. Choose great products, ones you're proud to represent and you'll soon be enjoying success in selling.

CHAPTER 7

Servicing to Succeed

How do you look after customers? Treat each of them as if they were your first! And do that by giving them the kind of service you like to receive when you are the customer.

I have stayed with the same hairdresser, doctor, dentist, accountant, and lawyer for years. Why? Because I stay with the ones who show me they enjoy dealing with me. Any relationship takes time to develop, and swapping and switching the people we deal with is no fun for either party. Be prepared to invest in building a solid relationship with every customer. Finding a new customer can take five times the cost, time, and energy it takes to keep an existing one, so don't let any slip through your fingers.

Keeping Customers with VIP Service

More people are driven away from a relationship than are lured away by the competition. People are driven away not by dissatisfaction of your product but by poor service.

We have to love our customers and let them know it. What's the opposite of love? While the word *hate* probably springs to mind, the opposite of love is actually indifference. How do you feel when you walk into a shop or restaurant, only to be treated as if you are invisible? Maybe there's someone on the desk more engrossed in paperwork or chatting to another staff member than looking up and making you feel special and welcome. How do you feel when you're put on hold when you're telephoning a company? You can't help feeling that if your call really "is important to us" they would answer it!

Research into customer service indicates that when people encounter bad service, few complain. Most just drift away and go some-where else.

48

To keep your customers you have to show them you value them. Aim to exceed their expectation, to delight them with your service. You won't be appreciated for just delivering what you promise. Only by surprising your customers and delivering more than they expect or have been used to receiving in the past will you truly demonstrate that you care.

How can you do this?

- Keep in touch regularly. If you miss them with your call, leave a message that you called and make sure you call back.
- List their favorites in your customer file and follow up at an appropriate time, such as when they are on special.
- Include a little hand-written note with each order, when it's delivered.
- Send a birthday card that you have individually selected for them.
- Recommend specific products they may like, based on information they have previously given you or your specific knowledge of their lifestyle.
- Make them feel special by giving them news quickly—new products, new developments—before they hear it secondhand from someone else. As your business grows, a regular Customer Newsletter can work well, especially if you have a computer. Keep it short, simple, and bright.
- Don't forget the power of a small thank-you gift from time to time. The value of the gift is less important than the gesture of appreciation. A short note is always a delight to receive.

We all like to be treated as special, and the best way to establish loyal customers is to treat each one like a VIP. When you make customers feel that dealing with them is the highlight of your day, it will surely be the highlight of their day, too!

Pursuing Excellence

Excellence is a moving target. Constantly ask yourself, "What am I doing right that I should continue, and what am I doing wrong that I could change or improve?" If you're not constantly improving, you're probably falling behind.

PLAN SERVICE TO THE PRODUCT

Set up a call cycle that best suits your product and stick to it. If your company is working on three-week or monthly campaigns, you'll want to fit in with this, at least.

It's a great idea to devise and follow a customer-servicing plan for each consumable product. Say, for example, you sell a nutritional supplement. Within a week, call the customer back and ask how she is finding the product.

Be genuinely interested because, (a) you should be, and (b) this will let you determine how many people in the family are taking the supplement and how frequently, so you can calculate how soon the product will be finished.

If you have sold one month's supply, make a day planner note to call your customer back and offer to order another. Call early enough to ensure delivery before the product runs out. It's your job to ensure her next purchase is your product again, and your commission. It's also a brilliant discipline to be in contact with your customers on a consistent, regular basis.

Even better, ask your customer's permission to place a regular order, to coincide with the product being finished (say, monthly). This is especially worthwhile if you are selling cleaning products, nutritionals, or skincare, which have easily tracked run-out times. Make your servicing call cycles of these products so consistent that buying from you becomes a habit. Then your customers will never even think of buying elsewhere. When you deliver, you're building regular business and you have an excellent opportunity to talk to your customer about another product in your range that may suit them or a new product release.

FIT SERVICE TO THE CUSTOMER

Always put your customer first. If they need a product urgently, do all you can to deliver. If they want to purchase small quantities, supply what your customer wants and can afford. This will bring repeat business and referrals, not requests for refunds! Think lifetime value, not short-term gain.

Every customer needs nurturing to develop their loyalty, but look what you know already about your customers that other retailers don't know, or rarely act on. You know their name, address, telephone number, family and personal interests. You know what products they have bought from you and enjoy using. How many times in your life have you had a personal, unprompted phone call from a retailer? You can have one with your customers every day.

You know your customer. Use this as your leading edge over other sellers. By comparison, the retailer is waiting for the customer to find a parking space and make it past the competitor further up the mall to his store; meanwhile, he's running up overhead paying the landlord and staff. Telemarketing and television sales generally offer a "one-size-fits-all" service, with little or no follow-up. And despite all the excitement the Internet has generated, currently less than 2 percent of people who enter the Internet looking to buy are actually making a purchase. Proof indeed that service, not price, still motivates people to buy.

Credit card safety and personal service will forever be your exclusive tools to outperform electronic, television, and traditional retailing. Use your strong relationship with your customer to optimize this advantage.

SUCCESS GROWS MOTIVATION

Don't drop the ball. If you do, your customers will lose confidence in you and go elsewhere. Retailers, malls, and other direct sellers are doing everything they can to get into your customer's wallet. The best way to beat them is with outstanding customer service.

As people begin to respond positively to you and the calls become easier, you'll find you gain more confidence and motivation.

When this happens you will discover one of the magical secrets of selling. No matter how many seminars you attend, how many books you read or motivational tapes you listen to, nothing motivates a salesperson like success!

Keep pushing until success comes and then you'll discover just how motivating, how addictive, it can be. If you find you're going through a flat spot, the only answer is to press on. A run of success will come back, together with the rush of motivation it brings.

Each success generates the next. Never treat a sale as a one-off, a one-time transaction. The commission on one sale is relatively small compared to the lifetime value of your customer.

For example, a product that lasts three months will produce four sales to the same customer in one year. That's 20 sales in five years. Compare the value of your commission when you multiply it by 20. That gives you an idea of the true value of the original sale. Each subsequent sale gets easier, as your relationship with your customer grows. Plus, you always have the potential to introduce a new product each time you make another sale of the original product.

ALWAYS FOLLOW UP

Never let a customer slip. After making the sale, follow up within two weeks to inquire how your customer is enjoying the product.

What's the worst thing that can happen? Your customer doesn't like it!

Well, if she doesn't like it, she won't be happy with it whether or not you call. If it does happen, offer to refund or replace (according to your company policy). No big deal! You can't please all the people all the time.

You'll get better word-of-mouth recommendations from a customer who is surprised at your positive response than one who is left with a product they're unhappy with and annoyed at not being able to return it.

What's more likely to happen? Your customer is happy, because you recommended the best product in the first place. They will be impressed by your consideration, your professionalism, your confidence in your product, and your ability to answer any questions about the product during your follow-up call. Your relationship will move up two notches and your next call to service and sell more products will be warmly received.

Always let your customers know, at the time of the first sale, that you intend following up to make sure they're happy with their purchase. During the follow-up call let them know you will be calling regularly. If you have a brochure or other literature you'd like to send, organize this during the call. "I would like to send you our monthly newsletter/catalog/leaflet/brochure. This way you'll be able to hear about new product releases and special promotions regularly. Is that okay with you?"

Never take your customer for granted, or someone else will take your customer. Never resort to excuses why you haven't called. ("Oh,

I've been so busy," or "The kids have been sick.") As nice as they are, customers care mostly about themselves. This is great, because when you demonstrate that you genuinely care about them, enjoy working with them, and appreciate their business, they're customers for life.

Apply "tough love" to yourself and make the calls. What's at stake in building a long-term customer base is credibility.

SET GOALS FOR ADDING TO YOUR CUSTOMER BASE

Depending on how quickly you want to build your business, aim to sign up an average of one new customer a day. That doesn't mean finding five customers in your first week and leaving it at that. It means setting a goal of finding one new customer every day, one day at a time, because this is the guaranteed way to earn the income and live the lifestyle you dream of.

When Your Business Grows

It's important to keep servicing your customers with follow-up calls even when your customer base is large. What happens when your business gets so big you can't possibly call everyone? When you get to this stage you can employ someone to help you. They call on your behalf. Pay them a flat rate per call (their income is a tax-deductible expense for you) with a bonus for achieving sales targets.

In addition to personal calls, most of the successful salespeople I know use the following system to manage and keep in touch with a large customer base. It's a simple six-step program to success:

1. Organize a merchant facility with the major credit cards in your area and include details on every order form to make it as easy as possible for your customers to purchase from you.
2. Arrange a "free post" or "post paid" facility and have envelopes printed with your name, address, and free-postage details.
3. Include an order form and envelope in every mailing. Whenever your customers receive mail from you it must be easy for them to choose products; complete their name, address, and credit card details; and place the preaddressed, prepaid envelope in

the return mail. The easier you make it for your customers to order, the more sales you will generate.

4. If appropriate, create a brief, topical customer newsletter, to accompany your leaflet or brochure. Keep your newsletter focused on making your customers feel valued and on making sales.

5. If possible, negotiate a special bulk postage rate with the postal service to take advantage of the savings available when you mail your customers in bulk quantities.

6. At least twice a year arrange an appointment with your customer for a personalized update on new products.

When you have built up a large customer base you'll find this kind of system works like magic.

The Magic Rings of Customer Service

Just like a magician with five interlocking magic rings, you will amaze your customers—and yourself—when you use these five tools every day in your business. However, unlike the magician, there are no hidden tricks. Each begins with the letter C to remind you that, like open rings, they can be easily linked together for excellence in customer service.

1. *Competence.* Be totally competent in your product knowledge, including benefits, prices, and service. Never stop learning about your products, about selling, about communicating, and about people. Be aware of your competitors and of trends in your industry.
   By subscribing to magazines in your field you'll be able to keep up with the latest news and trends. Search the Internet for information and ideas.
2. *Confidence.* Have confidence in yourself, your product, and your company. You are a walking, talking billboard for your business. Ensure that you are the best advertisement your business can have.
3. *Concern.* Be concerned about others' needs and interests— and show your concern. Learn how to put yourself in the other person's shoes, to think as they think. You won't get far in this business without empathy.
4. *Communication.* Communication is a two-way process. It's not what you say, it's what your customer hears that counts. Don't waffle, don't wander, don't confuse. Keep your messages uncluttered to give them a better chance of being clearly received.
5. *Courtesy.* No matter what, be courteous to everyone, even the most demanding customer. A courtesy call to inquire about how your customer is enjoying the product is always appreciated and will help build a strong relationship. It's not the situation but how you handle it that makes the strongest, most lasting impression.

Link your Competence, Confidence, Concern, Communication, and Courtesy rings together and your customer service will work like magic, as your customers keep reappearing.

How to Create a Customer Newsletter

Many successful network marketers build additional business with a regular customer newsletter.

It must be well conceived and well written to be appealing to read. Remember these basics:

- Include your name, address, and telephone details.
- Have topical content and interesting ideas relevant to your product, for example, tips for summer skin or top energy boosters. But keep it brief and to the point.
- Give a reason to purchase. Whether you adopt a recommendation or "specialing" approach, the purpose of your newsletter is to sell product, attract bookings, and intrigue potential recruits.
- Keep your typing accurate and your layout clean and uncluttered. Less is more! Always use your computer's spell-check tool and carefully proofread and double-check everything, especially prices, before printing.
- If you have time, personalize the copy you send to each VIP customer with a hand written note on it.
- Your company newsletters and flyers, or magazines relevant to your industry will always be a good source of information for you to pass on in your newsletter. Be sure to include appropriate credits.
- Sign off with a thank-you to your customers in advance, for their business.
- Don't forget the response order form, with payment details, preferably utilizing a credit card facility and the reply-paid envelope.

Once you have developed your newsletter, produce it on a regular basis. You'll be delighted how easy the newsletter makes it for you to build profitable, ongoing business from your existing customer base.

If you're on the Internet and confident with the technology, consider sending your newsletter as either an e-mail message or a document attached to a message.

CHAPTER 8

Working Your Business Makes It Work

Many network marketers do well at the start of their venture, because they have the initial energy, enthusiasm, and sales skills to make the first sales. But they falter because they lack the focus and discipline to work the system of regular calling.

Be the exception and you'll enjoy exceptional results.

Imagine working in a regular Monday-to-Friday, nine-to-five job, but staying away on payday, when you should be coming in to collect your check! Not servicing your customers with regular calling is exactly the same thing as not coming to work on payday.

It's the customers who fund your paycheck with their purchases. It's not the company who pays you, it's your customers. If you want to get paid, you have to call your customers.

Learn How by Doing

Much has been written about fear of following up, fear of the phone, fear of rejection, and fear of failure. Some degree of trepidation is perfectly normal, and we all have it.

There's only one way to overcome your reluctance and gain confidence: Hurdle the obstacle and master the skills. There is no other way! If you wait until you gain confidence before you do anything, you'll wait a long time. Learning comes from doing. You have to make the follow-up calls to your customers or you will have no business, or one built entirely from constantly drumming up new customers. This will keep you forever in the small league or quickly burn you out.

We may anticipate rejection over the phone, but how many times does it actually happen? If it does happen, what do you do? The same as the rider who's thrown from the horse, you get back in the saddle and ride again! There's only one way to do it. It's like learning to play the piano. The only way to learn to play the piano is to sit down at the keyboard and play the piano. Falteringly at first, then better, day by day, week by week, practicing until you become a virtuoso. You can't do it by reading books about it. You can't do it talking about it to your friends. You succeed by doing it over and over, until it becomes second nature.

Can you remember when you were a child, learning to ride a bike? You pedaled as hard as your little legs could, knowing you had the reassurance of a parent's hand to steady you. Then one day you were suddenly riding on your own, as they quietly took their hand away.

Remember the sudden surge, the feeling of accomplishment and freedom, soaring down the sidewalk?

You'll feel the same exhilaration when you overcome "call reluctance." Keep making the calls, and one day the feeling of fun and freedom will hit you, probably pushed along by your first big commission check!

Don't take rejection personally. I know, it's easy to say, but hard to live with. Remind yourself that you are not being rejected personally. They are only declining what you are offering and you already know that some will reject it.

The more you make the calls, the easier they become. Another thing happens, too. The more you make the calls, the more welcome your calls become.

Your reward will follow. Besides the money itself, there's the thrill of building a customer base and watching your business grow as you enjoy the glow of repeat purchases.

The Rewards and How You Get There

Many remuneration plans pay commissions up to 50 percent of the retail price to their top sellers. Make it one of your goals to keep building toward achieving the level where for every $100 in sales you keep $50 for yourself.

Try to see each customer at least twice a year. If you're working Party Plan and can turn this into a show, fine. Otherwise a 30-minute appointment (maximum) to introduce new products should be scheduled for every customer.

If you think this sounds time-consuming, look at the income it can earn for you.

I have based the following calculations on allowing 30 minutes for traveling (on average, because you always schedule several appointments in the same area), with each appointment taking no more than 30 minutes.

This means you can allocate one and a half days a week for customer appointments. Ten hours a week will enable you to manage 10 one-on-one appointments a week, or 500 a year. That's 250 customers, each seen twice, excluding those who book shows.

Calculate an average sale of, say, $40 per visit, or $80 a year from each of 250 customers. Your total sales will be $20,000. How much commission do you earn? If it's 50 percent, you earn $10,000 a year, or over $800 a month, for 10 hours' work a week, plus delivery. It's easy income, from existing customers!

Let's look at an illustration of the possible weekly workload for a person who works the business 30 hours a week, including Party Plan.

Weekly Activity	Average Sales	Time	Total Sales
10 one-on-one appointments	@ $40	10 hours	$ 400
3 Shows	@ $350	9 hours	$1050
40 telephone servicing calls	@ $15	4 hours	$ 600
Deliveries		3 hours	
Ordering and packing		3 hours	
Records and book-keeping		1 hour	
Total Weekly Hours Worked		30 hours	
Total Weekly Sales			$2050
Total Weekly Commission @50%			$1025

Follow this schedule and you'll be earning over $1,000 per week, or an annual income, before tax deductible expenses, of over $50,000 for just 30 hours' work a week.

Why would anyone even consider doing this part-time?

Whatever commission you're earning, do this exercise on your own figures. Some companies with higher priced products, such as fashion, children's clothing, and jewelry may pay lower commissions, but your average sale is usually higher, so the income balances out.

Practice What You Preach

Because network marketing works on the principle of duplication, practice what you preach and preach what you practice.

As you recruit others and build a business, your downline will follow your lead. Whether you're looking after 5, 50, or 500 customers, teach your downline, by example, the benefit of keeping in touch with every customer. Keeping in contact is the key to a successful business built on a base of satisfied, regular, and loyal customers.

It's when you set this example yourself, then recruit others to work full-time and duplicate your work ethic, that you build the business that will make you a millionaire. You won't make a million working only 30 hours a week. So what do you do with the rest of your time? You use it to grow your business by prospecting, interviewing, recruiting, training, and leading your downline. It's the synergy of many people working within your downline that builds the business for you.

Productive downline distributors not only add considerably to your income but also lead to higher level rewards, including dramatically increased bonuses, international trips, and company incentives such as jewelry and cars.

The point is, the more time you invest in your business, the more exciting your income becomes. But even if you work your network marketing business part-time and halve the time you invest, the income is still attractive if your activity is productive. You can analyze your business and determine exactly how much time to invest for the rewards you want.

The other main point to all this is the value of putting your focus on personal activity. There is always more power in what you do than what you say. Your downline should see that personal activity must be the basis of every successful network marketing business.

Delegate Responsibilities

If you find you're getting too busy, pay someone to take over deliveries—a courier service will work well—as this is the least productive part of your business (although every delivery is a chance to add customer service and introduce a new product).

Collating of orders can also be delegated. The small amount you pay someone else to do this—compared with the time it gives you to concentrate on selling and enjoying your family life—could be a good investment. Hopefully, your business will soon grow to the size where you can afford help with household chores. Pay your help enough and he or she could become a customer!

Say Thank You

Once a year, some of the most successful people I know hold VIP or customer-appreciation cocktail parties to recognize and thank their best and most loyal customers. Don't be too busy to show your appreciation. It's another way of investing in your business.

"Thank you" is a magical phrase in any language. This is another occasion where you can use your strength over retailers, direct marketers, and Internet traders. You know your customers. You know how to say thank you—in person.

Help Is on Hand

One of the realities of network marketing is that choosing your upline is about as difficult as choosing your parents. You may have a brilliant upline or, at the other extreme, you may find yourself out-growing your sponsor quite quickly.

If you honestly believe you don't have the right person as your upline sponsor, either look further up the line or ask your company for advice and support. We all need someone to teach us, to keep us on track, to help us. Look at how the world's top athletes and sports teams are supported by coaches, managers, motivators, trainers, and, today, sports psychologists. Ask any successful person and they'll attribute much of their success to the help and guidance they were given along the way.

Every training session and seminar you attend will allow you to meet those at the top. Seek them out and talk with them. In network marketing you'll find plenty of people willing to help you.

Look to others to give you ideas. They'll share stories that will help put your problems into perspective, because they have "been there, done that."

When you share your goals and your deadlines with a mentor they'll hold you to them. This is exactly what's required.

Work closely with your mentor and then, as soon as you can, turn around 180 degrees. Surprise! While you were busy looking to your upline for help, your downline team was looking for help from you. Give help as generously as it was given to you.

PART THREE

Building

Your Business

Base

CHAPTER 9

The People You Know

Your network marketing business will thrive through building and servicing your customer base, but it will become a multimillion-dollar operation only through recruiting people into your downline and training them in turn to build and service customers and to recruit and train new people to do the same.

The sooner you start duplicating yourself, and getting the people you recruit to do likewise, the sooner you'll start seeing impressive bonus checks.

Don't wait until you think you know the business before you start sharing the opportunity. Many successes come when a new person brings a friend along from the start. You learn and earn together, have fun and grow together.

Don't be concerned about being a student and a teacher at the same time. That's the way life is! The best teachers are constantly learning while sharing their experiences with others.

Start your business by creating a list of names to call and then start calling.

How Many People Do You Know?

How do you build a list of names?

How many friends do you have? Close friends, say 5-10. How many people do you know? Immediate family, say 10. Partner's family, say another 10. Relatives, 15, maybe 20. Other people you know, say 25. So, you probably know upwards of 75 people, right? It doesn't seem like many, does it? Let's throw in a few more to be optimistic, round up the figures and say you know 100 people.

Now we're in business, right? Wrong!

I have never done the final count of the number of people I know, but some experts say that if we're over the age of 21 we'll know 700 people. Others claim that if we're over the age of 25 we probably know up to 2,000 people, by name!

The point is, you know hundreds and hundreds of people! These people, people you already know, will form the basis of your prospecting list. They are your *warm list*, because you know them and they know you. Start writing their names down.

How Do You Recall All Their Names?

THE MAGIC PARTY

You need a memory trigger to find all those names in your head. I have found this one works like magic. Imagine you have just won $10 million in the lottery. You decide you'll spend some of your winnings on a party to celebrate your good fortune. The best party you could ever dream of. It's going to be a totally fantastic event.

There has never been a party like this. Fabulous food, champagne, entertainment, fun, and celebration. It's very easy to afford this party in your imagination.

You want to share the excitement with everyone you've ever met. You want everyone there. Family. Friends. Relatives. Old school friends. People with whom you used to work. People you have met through clubs, organizations, and church groups. Parents you've met from your children's school and other activities. Your hairdresser, your dentist, and the friendly nurse at the doctor's office. Everyone.

Start writing their names down.

Don't worry where they live. With your lottery winnings you can afford to fly them in from anywhere. Start looking for those old address books. Old Christmas card lists. Think of every area of your life. Start searching out old class photos and school yearbooks. Club membership lists. Business cards you threw in a drawer and forgot about.

Brainstorm with your family. Tell yourself you know 1,000 people. You just need help remembering all their names.

Write the names down in groups of 20. Each time you complete one group of 20 set yourself a goal of completing the next group.

You thought you hardly knew anyone, but you will be way past 100 before you start to get serious!

USING CATEGORIES

Use categories as thought-starters for your lists. Under each category, write down as many names as you can think of.

Try starting with my personal top 50 categories:

My best friends	Other friends
Friends from the past	Friends' friends
Old school friends	Partner's friends
Family members	Close relatives
Distant relatives	Partner's family
Neighbors	Previous neighbors
Coworkers	Previous coworkers
Partner's business associates	Business associates' partners
Parents of children's friends	Children's teachers
Retailers	Bank clerks
Hairdresser	Dry cleaner
Aesthetician	Florist
Staff at office supplies shop	Old address books
People met on a course	People met on vacation
Masseuse	Restaurant/coffee shop staff
Dentist/Dentist's assistants	Music teacher
Dance teacher	Doctor/doctor's staff
Sports club members	Health club members
Service club members	Librarian
Parents at children's clubs	Church members
Weight loss group	Baby sitter/cleaner
Gardener/maintenance person	Store check-out staff
Veterinarian/pet minder	Accountant/accountant's staff
Receptionists	Christmas card lists
Fellow students	Delivery people

Don't stop here. This is simply a list of thought starters. It shows you just how many different people you come across in your everyday life. Once you have listed names under each of these categories, think up your own categories and keep writing down the names.

They're in the Yellow Pages

Here's another magic trick that makes names appear out of thin air. Find the alphabetical index in the front of your telephone directory's Yellow Pages and use it as a prompt for categories. Scan through the listings, asking yourself, "Who works for an Accountant, is in Advertising, does my Alterations, works in the Antiques shop, is or works for an Architect . . ."

Go right through the index from A to Z. You may even be prompted to remember someone who works in the Zoo or studied Zoology. It's a great way of conjuring up names from out of the air!

Think in All Directions

You will be surprised how well prompts work. They trigger your memory and help you recall literally hundreds of people. You don't have to know every prospect.

Want to know how to turbo-charge the power of your prospect list building?

It's simple. Think of the next generation. Many of the people you've already listed have, or will have, one or more children or nieces and nephews reaching adulthood. Make a note now to always think upward, outward, and downward when you're adding to your prospect list.

Everyone Is a Prospect

You don't have to complete the list in one day or even one week. You don't even need address details or married names. That can all come later. At this stage, focus on getting the names down on paper. And most important, don't prejudge. Don't think "It's no good putting their name down, they'll never be interested." What if someone had said that about you? You are now about to start an exciting new venture with a warm list of potential customers and recruits already numbering in the hundreds, simply because someone thought to ask you.

How can you say anyone wouldn't like to hear about your new product and business opportunity, any more than you could say, "If I invited him or her to a party to celebrate my good fortune in winning the lottery, they wouldn't come."

For everyone who rejects your offer, you can be sure there will be another who will respond to you. You can't please all the people all the time, but the only way you will find the people you want is to ask.

Once you start doing it, you'll find it's not difficult to approach people in your community, from taxi cab drivers to optometrists to newsagents. Successful network marketers never stop meeting new people and adding new names to their prospect list.

Some companies use advertising to generate leads for their distributors. Others teach techniques that you can employ to create a database of people to call. However, spending money on advertising won't get you success. You're never going to build a million-dollar business unless you learn to generate your own leads, and, through your example, teach your downline to do the same.

Teach Your Recruits

As we've discussed, the key difference between direct selling and network marketing is duplication. Duplication is the magic that transforms your efforts into million-dollar results. And a basic principle of duplication is leading by example.

You will gain hours of precious time every week if you train your recruits to follow the examples you set in your own personal business. Take them with you to your shows, recruiting interviews, and personal consultations. Let them learn by observing you in action. There is no more powerful training situation than a live demonstration with a competent leader.

You can supplement your training with monthly meetings and encourage your recruits to take advantage of the many books, tapes, and magazines available to them.

How Do the Downline Numbers Work?

The figures below demonstrate how the downline numbers would work if, for example, you built your business using the magic factor of five. As shown in this hypothetical illustration, with each person at each level recruiting five people, your downline would be 3905 people after five levels:

First Level	5	Total Downline	5
Second level	25 (5x5)	Total Downline	30 (5+25)
Third Level	125 (25x5)	Total Downline	155 (30+125)
Fourth Level	625 (125x5)	Total Downline	780 (155+625)
Fifth Level	3125 (625x5)	Total Downline	3905 (780+3125)

Does the magic factor of five really work? Yes. And no. Because it's not as simple as it sounds. Human nature intervenes. People come and go. Yes, there are people in network marketing with downlines in excess of 10,000 people, (a Sixth Level on the above figures takes you to almost 20,000 people!) but there are others with a downline of just around 10 people. They are all working within the same parameters, but some are working harder and smarter. Even the numbers at the second and third levels can produce an exciting income.

You will see from the example how duplication involves both *width* and *depth*. Width represents those people you recruit directly, your First Level. Depth represents the people others recruit into your downline. The stronger you build width at the First Level, the better your chances of achieving depth as well. Most network marketing Remuneration Plans require a degree of width before you can be paid to any degree of depth, and bonuses paid to you may decrease at lower levels. It's best to build your First Level to more than the five given in this example.

CHAPTER 10

Making Your First Calls

You have created your list and now it's time to start setting up appointments to introduce people to your product or opportunity. The first step is to develop a discipline and a routine of calling.

Be Yourself

Have you ever answered your phone to the voice of a stranger asking, "How are you today?" I don't know about you, but it irritates me. Especially when they start to go through a scripted patter that sounds as if it has been prepared by someone else.

To sound sincere and natural, *be* sincere and natural.

Make your first cold call the same way you call any other friend. By being warm and being yourself.

Keep these points in mind:

- The purpose of your phone call is not to close the sale. You're asking for an opportunity to meet. Keep it brief.
- Always be honest and straight up. Explain your intentions. If you're excited and enthusiastic, this will come through over the phone.
- Imagine you are telling your friends about a movie you think they'll enjoy. Your tone will be just right.
- Personal endorsement is always powerful. For example, "Last winter it seemed someone in the house always had a cold. This winter, I had the whole family take these vitamins and guess what—no colds at all!"

Know What You're Going to Say

When you are making your first few calls, it's normal to feel a little nervous. I have made hundreds of presentations to audiences, from five people to over a thousand people, all around the world. Before each presentation, like every speaker I know, there are a few butterflies in my stomach. The secret is to get those butterflies flying in formation.

I have learned that writing out and rehearsing my first few sentences helps me enormously. Then writing the key points as headings allows me to cover everything in a naturally enthusiastic manner.

It's the same with your phone call. You'll find it easier if you know precisely what you want to say in your first few sentences. Write the sentences down and rewrite until you're happy.

Here's an example:

"Hello Samantha, it's Tiffany. I have just started my own business selling the most amazing range of cookware. I love it and can't wait to show you. Are you free for half an hour next Thursday after work?"

Don't fall into the trap of making it sound complicated. Follow my KISS principle—Keep It Short and Simple. Vary your approach, depending on how well you know the person you're calling. A good opener for someone you know well is ". . . and I thought of you first. I'd love to know what you think."

To approach people you admire, try, "When I saw the high caliber of people working with this company, I immediately thought of you." You'll find this style of gentle and sincere flattery will work.

If you or the person you're calling has been in network marketing before, say, "I learned a lot from my previous experiences and I am very confident this company is right for me. I think you will be impressed also."

Anyone who works for wages would have to give serious consideration to the question, "Do you think you are worth more than you are paid?"

Don't be apprehensive about approaching friends and family. They are the first people you'd call if you opened a new shop or restaurant. It's no different in network marketing. You're opening your own business and friends and family will expect your call and love to hear about your exciting new venture.

Before you make any call, think through what you are going to say. Check your written opening—but don't "read" it over the telephone.

Knowing what you want to say will help you relax and you'll come across confidently.

Keep your enthusiasm to a level that will intrigue. "I can't be sure this will appeal to you, but it is so exciting I'd love to chat with you about it over a coffee." Never force the other person into a corner, but give them an "out", that will allow them to decline gracefully.

You'll find your confidence attracts other people who want to be around you and become involved in your business.

Some Don'ts

When you're on the telephone making a cold call, watch out for these common mistakes:

- *Overselling.* Don't overwhelm your prospect with your urgency and need to succeed. Be bright and enthusiastic, but not overpowering or belligerent.
- *Talking too much.* Remind yourself that the purpose of this call is to get an appointment, not make a sale. My recommendation is to stick to one or two compelling points. You want to intrigue your prospect enough to meet with you.
- *Showing little interest in or empathy with your prospect.* Take the time to ask questions, listen to and think about the answers. The more you know about your prospect, the better equipped you will be to make a successful connection. Show a genuine interest in the person you're calling.

The secret of a cold call? Be warm. Be yourself. Keep it short and simple! And no matter what the outcome of the call, don't forget to say thank you.

Prospecting for Gold

Prospecting is the lifeblood of your business. If you find the thought of making a lot of calls daunting, think of yourself as panning for gold. The gold prospector knows that what he's after is somewhere in among all the sand. He takes one pan full of sand, then another, and another, sifting through it until he finds the gold he's looking for. There is no shortcut to this sifting process.

If the pan doesn't produce gold, the prospector doesn't resift the same sand, hoping one day he will find gold. Rather, he moves on to a fresh load, knowing if he keeps sifting new sand, sooner or later he will find flecks of gold and, from time to time, the rare gold nugget.

You'll find that about 1 percent of your recruits turn out to be the rare gold nugget—people just like you who know what they want and are prepared to do what it takes to achieve it. Keep looking for them.

One of the most frequent errors of judgment I see in this business is someone focusing their attention and expectations on people they have already worked with unsuccessfully. If you keep working with the same people, you're not going to improve your results. The only answer is to be constantly finding new people. The more people you sift through, the greater your chances of striking gold! Keep sifting new sand.

There are no shortcuts.

CHAPTER 11

By Appointment Only

Successful network marketing people target 20 names a day for appointments. Five minutes a call is plenty of time to make your point and still have a friendly chat. Twenty calls at five minutes will take less than two hours a day. The successful network marketers know they must make 20 daily calls and of the 20, many will turn them down. A 20 percent success rate seems to be the network marketing average for making an appointment to sell your product or business opportunity.

Calls = Appointments

Nothing is more essential in network marketing than a day planner full of appointments. If you want to have four appointments a day, you will have to call at least 20 people from your list daily. Before you start calling, take the time to find each phone number and address. Do this step first, filling out your list, so when you start calling you don't break your rhythm to look up these details. You can focus on making the calls, without the interruption of searching for elusive phone numbers.

Then, start calling. Without an overload of detail, talk in simple, enthusiastic terms about the company and the key reason why you have chosen to be involved with the products.

The following examples, for a variety of product lines, show it is simple to make your point with natural enthusiasm.

> *Children's clothing:* "Children adore the designs, and the fabrics can be washed over and over and still look good."
> *Cookware:* "You won't believe how much fun I'm having in the kitchen now. And it's such outstanding quality that every item has a lifetime guarantee."

Jewelry: "You'll love our original designs. Each piece is crafted in the company's own workshop, so the prices are lower than you'd expect for the quality."

Long-distance calling: "Our family's spread across the country, so it has always cost us a fortune in calls. Now we can afford to talk whenever we want to."

Nutritional supplements: "I can't believe how much more energy I have now that I am taking these supplements."

Weight loss products: "I've lost weight before, but have never been able to keep it off the way I can now."

Whatever your product, involve your customer or recruit very early on in the call by relating how the products or the opportunity will specifically appeal to them.

Appointments = Success

A basic principle of network marketing is that the more time you spend face-to-face with others, the more your business will succeed, so always ask for an appointment. "Let's make a time for coffee now. I can't wait to see what you think."

When you are starting out, family, close relatives, and good friends will respond to a statement such as, "This is all new to me, so please let me practice on you. I would value your feedback on how I'm doing." Try sharing the excitement of your new venture by telling them, "I must have 10 bookings before I can start and I hoped you would be one of them."

Some companies require a certain number of bookings before you start, and it's an excellent discipline, as without bookings in your day planner you have no business. Whether or not your company requires it, at least 10 start-up appointments in your first month must be your personal minimum goal. The stronger your start-up month, the more quickly your business will gain momentum.

Perseverance = Momentum

It's worth working hard to develop momentum because it creates a magnetic energy that attracts other people to you and your business. If you find your momentum slowing after the first month or so, simply remind yourself you're already on your way to making your first million dollars from your business and step up your efforts.

Make a conscious decision not to be unnerved or upset by negative responses. Expect them, because they are an inevitable part of the business. Tell yourself that *no* is not the same word as *never*. If you are polite, courteous, and friendly you will always be welcome back later.

Don't let a run of poor responses dishearten you. Persevere and you will be rewarded with success. Sooner or later, a good run will come. One good recruit who goes on to become a star in your downline can make a dramatic difference to the overall picture of your business. Part of being successful means being prepared to get turned down along the way. When you know the hurdles are going to be there, you don't let them trip you.

You'll find your success rate increases as you gain more experience. There are two reasons for this. First, you start to learn what works and what doesn't and, second, you become more relaxed and self-confident. Other people pick up this confidence subconsciously. They will relax and be more receptive to your message.

If you feel you are getting too few appointments, have the courage to question the technique you are using. Vary your call until you find an introduction that works. Being prepared for a high rejection rate allows you to experiment until you find a way of expressing yourself that gets results. Learn to change things around to suit different personalities. We can't change other people, only ourselves. The most successful business builders constantly review, and, if necessary, revise their approach. Ask for help from the person who sponsored you, perhaps inviting them to listen while you make the calls and give guidance.

Believe me, you will get better with practice. We learn by doing. The more calls you make, the more confidence you will gain. Success will follow. Keep making the calls.

I cannot overemphasize that without appointments in your day planner you have no business. No one is likely to call you asking to buy your products or discuss the business opportunity. You have to make your list, make the calls, and get the appointments.

If you become a little concerned about the amount of time and energy you're putting in at the beginning, think of yourself as a space rocket. Rockets use more energy in taking off and clearing the earth's gravitational pull than in traveling a million miles and returning to earth. It's only natural to put in the extra effort to get your business off the ground. The more fire power you put in at the beginning, the higher you are going to soar and the longer you'll stay at a high altitude.

Handling Rejections

Your initial goal is to call 100 people. When one says, "no thanks" remind yourself that was only 1 percent—that's nothing. However, none of us likes to be rejected. One way of coping is to put this rejection into a tidy little "package" that you can dispose of easily. I have heard many successful network marketing people chant a little mantra to themselves after rejection: "Some Will, Some Won't, So What, Who's Next?"

They have learned that the ones who say no don't count. They know they have to sort through them to find the ones who say yes and every rejection shortens the path to a "yes" response.

Be prepared to press on. Overcoming your feeling of rejection is the hardest part of the business. Master it and you gain a skill that will form the basis of your future success. Most of the people who fail at network marketing do so because they give up after a few unsuccessful calls, never getting on their feet again. As with most ventures, it's those who press on after stumbling at the first hurdles who are successful and reap the rewards of their success.

Don't give up. If you're getting a 20 percent success rate you may have to make 100 calls to get 20 appointments or bookings. Accept the rejections as part of building your customer base and your business. Keep making the calls, experimenting with different approaches, until you develop the ones that get the best results.

Discipline Is the Key

A good discipline is to close yourself in a room and stay there until you have completed your day's quota of calls. Give yourself a little reward for each 20 calls you make. I promise making these calls at the start of your business is the toughest part. Overcome call reluctance, make the calls one at a time, and you're on your way to success.

Many of the leaders in this industry encourage their new recruits to agree to a time when they will make those all-important first calls. The leader telephones just before the scheduled time to wish the new recruit luck and quickly preview the calls, then telephones again immediately after with congratulations if the exercise has been successful, or to give a review with guidance and encouragement if a less than successful result has been achieved.

Some successful network marketing leaders help their new people by literally shutting them in a room in their own house and encouraging them not to come out until they have made the calls.

This sounds like tough love, and it is. There are no shortcuts. To get the results you have to make the calls. When you bring new recruits into your business, you do them no favors by taking a casual approach to this critical process.

Experienced network marketing people teach their downline that disciplined calling works for two reasons: (a) because it does work and it's how you build your business, and (b) because they are also teaching the downline how to teach their own downline when the time comes. This is a key point, as in network marketing we learn by doing. From day one, your new recruits are building the habits that will make or break their business. It's up to you to help them learn the habits that you know will increase their chances of success.

The more interest you show in your new recruit, the more encouragement and support you give, the better the result will be. Using this approach guarantees the calls will be made, as the expectation has been set.

The Tricks of Telephone Time

The telephone is a key tool to network marketers. Learn to love it because you're going to be using it a lot. Until you overcome any reluctance to use it, your potential to build your business is limited. These techniques work:

- Schedule telephone time and stick to it. Don't allow any other activity to encroach on your telephone time.
- Move away from distractions. Children, the radio or television, or others talking will distract you, and the person you're calling will notice. I like to lock myself away, as closing a door puts me into my own totally focused world.
- Keep calls short. Be warm but don't fall into the chat-trap. If you want to make 100 calls a week, that's 20 every day, day in, day out, five days a week. Keep your calls short or you'll never achieve your target. Keep each call to five minutes and the entire process will take less than two hours a day.
- Don't oversell. When you meet, you'll be able to spend time getting to know the things that interest your customer or intended recruit. You can then manage your conversation to include the points you want to make, from their point of view.
- Smile. No matter how you're feeling, how you're looking, how you're dressed, the only thing the person on the other end of the telephone can "see" about you—even on a bad-hair day— is the smile in your voice. If you feel you're not coming across brightly enough on the phone, place a mirror next to it and draw on a happy face. Or stick your happiest photo by the phone. These work as prompts to always be and sound happy.
- Try this little game: Set your target of 20 calls today. Place two bowls beside the telephone, one empty, the other containing 20 children's marbles, M&Ms, small coins, or something similar. Each time you complete a call, transfer one from the full bowl to the empty bowl. There's nothing like the honest reality of six counters left in the "calls-to-make" bowl to remind you to keep phoning! And don't forget to reward yourself when you achieve your quota.
- Always have fun and, no matter what the outcome, make sure your call has improved the other person's day.

CHAPTER 12

The Power of Referrals

There's another form of gold waiting to be discovered among everyone you contact—referrals.

You may not agree with social psychologists who say each of us knows 2,000 people. But even if you called, say, only 100 people, and each gave you one lead from all of the hundreds of people they know, you will have another 100 people to call. In reality, they'll probably give you two or three leads, and these are the precious material required for building your business.

Ask Who They Know—and Who Else

When I relocated to North America I knew no one. In the weeks prior to my departure I chatted to everyone about how excited I was by the new challenge. I asked if they knew anyone in North America who could be interested in the business. Less than a week before I left New Zealand, while having a last-minute dental checkup, I asked my dentist (no easy task with a mouth full of apparatus). He suggested I contact a friend of his in Vancouver. I did, we met and within months she had the fastest growing business for that company in North America. The lesson is you never know where you are going to find the nugget of gold unless you keep finding new sand to sift. So when you talk with referrals, ask them for referrals, too.

The key to getting new leads is to ask, "Who else do you know who might be interested in this product/opportunity?" When they give you a name say, "Thank you, can you think of someone else?" Two easy questions that will pump life into your business.

Although your list of referrals will be people you haven't met, when you call them it won't be a total cold call. Telephone them and say, "I was chatting with our mutual friend Beki the other day and she suggested I give you a call because . . ." The ice is already broken.

The Party Plan

At this point I will declare my enthusiasm for the Party Plan style of selling. With Party Plan, you present your product or opportunity in a *show* or *workshop* to a group of people. Nothing beats shows for making bookings and recruitment appointments. The guests at a show already know the benefits of direct selling, they are warm to the concept (they're at the show, aren't they!) and they enjoy socializing. Plus, they're experiencing firsthand the process and rewards involved.

At a show, ask guests to host one for their own friends. This helps you break out from one circle of people and break into new ones. Party Plan companies offer gifts or incentives to reward those who hold a show, so always talk about the rewards that can be achieved when a show is held. If people are going to hold shows for you, or join you in the business, it will be because they are interested in the incentives, or the income. Be open and up-front about the exciting rewards available.

Shows are one of the best ways to build momentum in your new business. If, for every show you hold, you book at least one more, your day planner will always be full. What a wonderful feeling! Many successful Party Planners have the goal of "For every show held, get two more." As up to 50 percent of shows booked can be postponed or canceled, this is an excellent target. Keep reminding yourself to ask for ongoing bookings until it becomes a habit.

While Party Plan doesn't suit all product lines, I believe that if you use the dynamics offered by a group you will achieve success faster and easier.

Never Stop Looking for New Leads

Whether you're selling one-to-one, Party Plan, or both, I cannot overstate the importance of asking for ongoing bookings and referrals. Your business will grow only when you are constantly looking for new business leads. A one-on-one discussion could lead to an appointment that in turn could lead to another. A business interview could lead to an invitation to present the opportunity to three or four friends.

Ongoing referrals pump life into your business. Network marketing works if you do, and you have to keep working at getting referrals.

The alternative to working this system is failure. Without referrals and ongoing bookings you will work through your first list of people until finally . . . you hit the wall. You reach the end of your original list and run out of names (more people are going to say "No thanks" than "Yes please"). To build your business, it's essential that you constantly have a list of new names to call. You're not going to be like the retailer, hoping someone is going to come to you. Your business is calling people, getting to know them, finding out how your products and opportunity will benefit them. That's why network marketing is often called relationship marketing and why you have to use your original contacts to feed and grow a new list.

You can never have too many names. If you ever did find yourself overbooked, you could always share leads with your top recruits. However, resist the temptation to give leads to those you think need them. Always direct leads to your best people, the ones who have proven they have what it takes to do justice to the lead.

Think of your first list of names as your inner circle of contacts. Referrals are the only way to break out beyond that inner circle to the abundance of prospects beyond.

The good news is that every new person you call has a similar circle of friends. You break into new circles by asking, each and every time, "Who else do you know who might be interested in this product/opportunity? Thank you, can you think of someone else?" Adding a request for referrals to your customer order form will also help. Reward each successful referral with a small gift or, at the very least, a thank-you note.

Go Back to Your List

Don't forget you still have those uncalled names on your original list, which, by thinking and talking with family and friends, will keep growing way past the 100 you called during your first week in business. Keep brainstorming with your family and friends to remember the names of people you have known in the past. Plus—and this is the bonus of being focused—you will now find yourself always meeting new people. Once you open yourself up to them, you'll discover opportunities are always all around you.

Where to Meet New People

Perhaps you have just relocated to a new area and feel you don't know enough people. Where do you find them?

- Join a community service, hobby, or activities club. Toastmasters is excellent because you meet new people and it helps you build speaking and leadership skills. Don't be put off because you think you're not a good speaker. It's not a speaker's organization, it's a club for people who want to become better speakers.
- Go to adult community education classes.
- Join a gym or neighborhood jogging group.
- Get involved on school committees or volunteer to help out at your local school. Help is always appreciated and it's a great way to meet new people.
- Join a church group and involve yourself in their activities.
- Join a theater group. Even if you don't have acting skills, there is always a need for people to sell and collect tickets, help as ushers, prepare the sets, locate the props, and make the coffee.
- Volunteer for charity work.
- Organize a stand or display at a trade show.
- If you have preschool children, join a play group to meet other mothers.
- Ask the management of your local mall if you can rent a booth for a short-term promotion.
- Knock on your new neighbors' doors and introduce yourself. They will know you have recently moved in and will be interested to meet you and learn about your business.
- Do a mailing in an area close to your home. Your company may have suitable literature to personalize with your name and contact details. Add an incentive offer for people to call you within a certain time frame. Make the mailing a family project.
- Open up to the people you deal with on a daily basis, at the local store, the dry cleaner, the bank, the bakery, the library, the coffee shop, telling them about your career.

- Place a notice on your community notice board, cafe notice board or in a shop window. Try to put notices where your market is. For example, if you're selling nutritional or weight-loss products, try getting notices into fitness centers.
- Advertise in your local newspaper. Be prepared to run the advertisement for several weeks. It can take some time for people to respond. Repetition works, as does an incentive to call.
- Work with your company to have your own home page, preferably linked to the company's Web site.

You'll find network marketing is a great way to get to know people and assimilate into your new community. But nothing will happen unless and until you make it happen. It's up to you.

Why Do You Need New People?

Your business needs a constant flow of new people coming into it to be an ongoing success. You won't become a success, let alone make your first million, without new people coming into the business constantly. As well as finding new people through your own efforts, convey to your recruits the importance of new people for their success.

New people:

- Increase your immediate and future income
- Generate life and enthusiasm
- Help you achieve higher status levels and incentives
- Bring new ideas, skills, diversity, and contacts
- Increase momentum and energy as numbers swell
- Increase your security through a bigger base of people
- Produce stability by replacing those leaving or failing
- Set the right example to your downline.

Running a successful network marketing business means being a successful recruiter. To keep your business alive, you can never stop finding new people. They will be your business's life force. Make recruiting an everyday activity, until it becomes a way of life.

CHAPTER 13

Your People Files

Everything's going as well as you dreamed, hoped, and planned. Then suddenly . . . you feel out of control. It was fine when you only had a handful of customers or a small downline, but now you feel as if your head is bursting.

Help is required.

The answer is simple; the one every successful network marketing salesperson uses, from their first day in business.

Your *People File*.

Think what happens when you visit your doctor. At the beginning of your appointment the doctor reviews your file, checking your previous visits, symptoms, ailments, and treatments to be totally up-to-date with your entire medical history.

Now, let's turn the tables. You are the professional.

Build your files on your computer, or with a simple, inexpensive card index system, available from most stationery suppliers.

The Customer File

Let's start with your Customer File. For each new customer, complete a card or computer file. Write down everything you have learned about them. Name, address, and phone number. Partner's name. Children's names and ages. Birthdays. Interests. Sports. Include memory-joggers from information you gathered when they were talking and you were listening.

Your card index system will have a series of blank dividers that allow you to file your customer cards alphabetically or by call cycle.

Use your Customer File conscientiously. Always update it as you learn more about your customer and they start buying regularly.

Record what they buy from you. What their favorite products are. Problems they have that could be solved with products your company may bring out in the future.

As your business grows, you can't be expected to remember everything. Next time you visit your doctor, take a glance at the size of your medical history. You'll be amazed. Nothing happens that is not added to your file. It has to be the same way with your business, too.

Once you build and maintain your Customer File, you can use it other ways, too. You have listed your clients from A to Z. Now write out a month of "date" section dividers, from the 1st to the 31st.

Here's how it works. You sold Rena a bottle of shampoo on Tuesday the 7th, so you plan to follow up a week later. Take Rena's card from her alphabetical listing and place it behind the divider for Monday the 14th. That day, you pull up and review the card, call Rena, chat about her husband, Richard, and her son, Robbie—and the shampoo. As part of your customer service you inquire about the purchase, reinforcing the product's benefits.

"How are you finding the shampoo? Doesn't it leave your hair feeling wonderful?"

If she has not yet started to use it (perhaps she has not finished the bulk bottle she bought at the supermarket) use your call as an opportunity to reinforce to her the benefits she can expect. For example, more volume, more body, more shine.

Update Rena's card, return it to the file, putting it, say, behind the divider for Monday the 28th. Then, in two weeks time, the card will automatically remind you of your next follow-up and details of your previous call.

When you use this system, your customers will appreciate the interest you take in them. They'll be impressed because you can recall enough about them to make them feel special, which in turn makes them feel that you are special.

It's been said that people don't care how much you know, until they know how much you care. By recalling details about your customers and their lives you can show you care. By writing the details down, you'll be able to recall them later and show your interest in your customers.

The Downline File

As you build your downline, you will create your Downline File the same way. Include all the same personal details, but don't forget to include milestones, achievements, key dates, and other little reminders to yourself that will help you work effectively with everyone in your team.

The Heart of Your Business

Discipline yourself to use your Customer and Downline Files as a regular routine. Consistently update them to keep on top of your business.

They are the heart of your business. Just as your doctor has your health history in his medical files, you have the good health of your business in your Customer and Downline Files.

When you are ready for it, keeping your files on your PC will save you a lot of time and effort. A computer will make it quick and easy to pull up each individual history, as well as enabling you to create personalized letters in bulk, print labels, keep your financial records in order and communicate through e-mail and fax.

But, whether you're using a computer or a card file, it's the same system, the same information. The only difference is the way it's filed.

PART FOUR

Developing

Your

Downline

CHAPTER 14

Presenting the Opportunity

The time to start building your downline is immediately after you sign up. There is never a more powerful time to recruit than when you are beginning your business. If there is a hard and fast rule of building a downline, it's this:

Go hard and go fast.

Think of yourself as a talent scout always on the lookout for potential recruits. Your high level of enthusiasm will be contagious. Use it to great effect in presenting the business opportunity to recruit others into your team.

The speed at which you build your network marketing business will be in direct proportion to how quickly you can learn and apply the skills of recruiting, training, and leading your team.

You're enthusiastic because you have seen that it works. Don't worry about your lack of experience. You and your team can develop together, learn together, and earn together.

How Do You Sell an Opportunity?

Selling the business opportunity is the same as selling your products, except you're talking about something that will be created in the future.

That's why it's referred to as an opportunity.

When I say selling the opportunity, the reality is that in network marketing you *sell* the product, but *give* the opportunity. Just as someone gave you the opportunity, now it's your turn to give it to others.

Everyone is different. Some people are attracted to network marketing strictly for the money. Others will respond to the lifestyle benefits or because they dream of driving their first brand-new car, paid for by the company. Plenty of people find the international seminar travel irresistible. Some join because of a strong love of or belief in the product. Don't underestimate the fact that some people will join because they admire you and want to be a little more like you, by doing what you do.

How to Cold-Call a New Prospect

Just how do you start your first cold call to someone new? The best advice I can give you is to be yourself. The following conversation is not a script; it is an outline of how such a conversation might go. You may find it helpful, as a guideline to developing your own approach.

"Hi there, my name is (*use your first name or first name and surname*). I am hoping you may be able to help me. I represent a company called (*your company name*) and I'm looking for people to promote (*your product—for example, 'high-quality nutritional supplements'*) in this area. Do you know anyone who might be interested in earning a part-time or full-time income, working from home?"

It is likely you will be asked a few questions. Answer briefly, moving the conversation back to them. Ask, "What kind of work do you do? Do you have a family? How many children? What do you do for fun? Does the idea of earning extra money interest you?"

Show your prospects that you are genuinely interested in them. Find out more about them and you'll discover that they will return your interest by asking more about you and the business you're involved with.

How to Present the Opportunity

Once you have made the appointment, the basic steps in presenting the opportunity are the same as selling the product:

- Building a relationship
- Finding the hot buttons that will motivate your prospect
- Sparking interest based on those hot buttons
- Overcoming barriers that can get in the way
- Getting the agreement signed
- Following through

Now let's look at the process piece by piece.

Building the Relationship

Show a genuine interest in the other person. Learn to dig deeper when questioning, by responding to an answer with another question on the same subject. For example, "This is a lovely home. How long have you lived here?" would be followed by "Where did you live before that?" then "What prompted you to move?" or "How do you enjoy living here?"

Discovering Hot Buttons

Use the questions we talked about earlier for finding out what makes people tick. To find out what interests, motivates, and drives your prospect, ask questions that will tell you:

- What their dreams and goals are
- How prepared and committed they are to achieving a quality lifestyle
- What commitments, needs, or pressures they have
- What they know about your product, your company, and the network marketing industry
- How much time they have available to invest in building a business
- How high their level of interest is

Sparking Interest and Overcoming Barriers

Start along the following lines: "Dane, thanks for meeting with me so we can chat more about what I mentioned over the phone. What I want to talk about is the opportunity to set yourself up in your own business. I'll explain briefly about the company, the products, and how easy it is to promote them.

"This isn't for everyone, so if you decide it's not for you, that's fine. But I called you because I think starting your own business would appeal to you. If you like what I show you, I will help you get started. The decision is yours, of course."

You'll notice that this introduction presents the opportunity from the other person's point of view. Don't make the mistake of rushing in all enthusiastic about the company and the products. Your prospect will be wondering, "What's in it for me?" Make sure you present everything to fit that perspective before moving to a 15-minute overview of the company, the products, and the remuneration plan. Allow time to discuss any questions and objections your prospect may raise.

Throughout your presentation, build and maintain a high level of genuine enthusiasm and excitement about their interest. Tell them of your desire and availability to help them and keep expressing confidence that they will be successful. In return, make sure your prospect is willing to commit to the business. A commitment is a promise to do what it takes to make it work.

Here are some basic guidelines to follow when presenting your opportunity:

- Be up-front and honest. Long-term businesses are built on integrity.
- Don't oversell. There is no need to. Your products, your company, and your opportunity will sell themselves without the need for exaggeration. Unrealistic expectations will quickly lead to disillusionment and a rapid exit from the business.
- Don't pressure people. Accept "No thanks" or "Not for me, thanks" gracefully. This leaves the door open for the future and for referrals.
- Don't overpromise. The best advice I can give you is to not overdeliver on your promises. When you exceed expectations you build loyalty and trust.

Remember that, while you can't control how many people accept your offer, you can control how well and how often you present it. Consider the change network marketing has made to your life and how you now have the power to change other people's lives.

If you find your prospect slipping toward "Perhaps," when you thought they were a definite new recruit, you may want to ask to see them again, with their spouse or partner. Encourage questions and objections while you are together, so you can appreciate their concerns and provide positive answers. If necessary, arrange for them to meet your sponsor, or perhaps invite them to an opportunity function, where the business is presented formally.

CLOSING

Close with a definite next step. If a decision is not made on the spot, confirm when you will be in touch to discuss it further.

If the prospect accepts the opportunity, always explain what you will be doing to support them and help them get started. Your new recruit will be excited by the big picture but must understand that the process is a series of small steps.

Match every task with a timetable and use small incentives or rewards, such as demonstration products or sales aids, for a successful result. Recognizing and celebrating successes, both small and large, is an integral part of your network marketing leadership.

If your prospect turns you down, always leave the door open. Things change. Someone who is not interested today could be in totally changed circumstances in six months. People are made redundant at work every day. Whether it's your prospect or their partner who loses a job, today's conversation could take on a whole new perspective in six months' time. A thank-you note, whatever the outcome, will stay in their minds until the timing is right.

And when the "no, thanks" or "perhaps" turns into a "yes," a warm note of welcome to your new recruit will set the tone for a long and happy relationship.

Start Now!

I cannot overstate the importance of starting to build your downline from your first day in network marketing. The most powerful time to recruit is when you are fresh and at your most enthusiastic. The sooner you start, the sooner you learn to be successful at recruiting. Don't wait until you are more experienced. Starting now is the only way to gain experience!

CHAPTER 15

Bringing Your Customers into Your Downline

At some stage, most successful people in business attribute their success to having a mentor, a person who believed in them and helped them toward their success. Your success will come from duplicating yourself, from being an inspirational leader and mentor to others, and from helping others toward their own highest level of achievement.

The more you help others to be successful, the more successful you will be.

When you're looking for recruits, start with your existing customers. Just as they are your strongest source of referrals for sales, they are also your best prospects for recruiting into the business.

They know you and like you. They know your product and like it. They have heard about the training and support you were given. They have seen your development and your success. All they may be waiting for is to be invited.

Listen and Plant Seeds

Your customers have probably noticed you're making money while having fun. The idea grows in their head that they could be doing it, too. But nothing grows unless a seed is planted.

As you learn to do more listening than talking, you'll hear many opportunities to plant seeds. If you are too much of a talker, you won't even notice these opportunities.

If you're not sure if you talk too much, stop talking and try listening instead, and see how much better your business becomes!

A common topic of conversation is the employment situation. You may be talking with someone who is finding it difficult to get the right job, or having a problem getting back into the work force after time off from raising a family.

This gives you a good opportunity to talk about the unexpected things that happen in life, including people getting laid off due to company mergers, restructuring, or downsizing. When you explain how your network marketing business has enabled you to achieve security, develop personally, and advance professionally, your prospects will see the value in the opportunity offered to control their own destiny.

When you hear people complaining about their jobs or their bosses, show empathy. Talk about how few of us are happy with our work, and then describe why you are happy with yours. Tell them about how much you make per hour, the freedom, the lifestyle, the company paid trips and other rewards that are on offer, and the company car, if appropriate.

If you sense someone is feeling vulnerable in their current position, talk about how the smartest solution is to create your own job security. And don't forget to mention other benefits that come with being self-employed in network marketing.

Some women, after raising a family, feel the working world has changed and left them behind. Many accept jobs well below their level of skill, education, employment experience, and potential. When you mention the training and support you are given and how people come into the business from many different backgrounds, you'll be planting productive seeds.

You may hear women talking about the difficulty and expense of finding quality childcare during working hours. This is when you can plant the seed of network marketing couples working together. One is at home during the day while the other is at work; then they swap over a couple of nights a week, with one out meeting customers and doing shows while the other is at home looking after the children. The flexibility of network marketing can allow parents to be at home for their children after school and to join them in leisure and sporting activities, while still succeeding at their network marketing business.

When someone says you look confident and at ease doing your presentation, tell them that when you started you didn't know anything about the product. Use the company's training as a seed to reiterate how easily they could learn the business and achieve what you are achieving.

When people tell you they're too busy to do something like this, they might really be asking, "How would I find the time?" Empathize with how they feel; tell them you felt the same way at first. Then relate how you found that the busier you became, the easier it was to become better organized. The fact is, busy people make brilliant recruits, as they have the energy and drive to succeed.

The skill with seeds is to plant them and carry on with your presentation.

Problems with Spouses or Partners

If they say their husband, wife, or partner probably wouldn't like them spending so much time away from home, agree. Tell them yours had the same reservation, until the commission checks started coming in. The reality is that most families today will benefit from any extra income that can be earned.

For some women there can be a potential problem with husbands or partners who don't take their business seriously, or feel resentful at their new income and sense of independence.

It's not for me to comment on personal relationships, but the lessons I have learned from watching others grow in network marketing are reflected in the words written by Shakespeare: *This above all: to thine own self be true."*

I believe we each have a challenge in life to fulfill our personal destiny. When you have the courage to be the success you know you can be, problems inevitably seem to solve themselves.

Try to involve a partner at the earliest possible stage, even the initial interview, as they will often become less defensive and more supportive. They feel involved in that their views are respected and they hear about your business firsthand.

Feeling Secure

To me, there's real disappointment in the willingness of so many people to accept poorly paid, unchallenging, and inflexible jobs for the reason of so-called security. For these people, the highlight of the day is quitting time. And yet the so-called security of this kind of job often vanishes in the first corporate restructuring.

By contrast, there are many wonderful opportunities in network marketing to feel secure and enjoy your work, to meet new people, and have fun, while earning three or four times your previous hourly rate.

Network marketing offers true reward for your efforts. It provides challenge, excitement, travel, freedom and the opportunity for dramatic personal development in both skills and self-confidence.

Don't miss any chance to offer this magical lifestyle to everyone you meet.

Your Business Opportunity Kit

Never leave home without having your sponsoring tools with you. Your company will supply you with appropriate sponsoring or recruitment tools and literature. Collate the relevant material, together with agreement forms, contracts, and your business cards, into an Opportunity Kit.

Read and reread all the material until you become completely familiar with it. Learn how to complete the forms. Know what the company requires in the way of payment, what payment terms are available, and what taxes and delivery charges apply. Know the requirement for advance bookings and what incentives are currently on offer to encourage new recruits.

You never know when someone is going to say yes and you don't want to be caught without the knowledge or the material.

As a leader, recruiting isn't part of your job, it *is* your job.

CHAPTER 16

Where Do You Find the HIPO?

Your business will need *HIPOs*. We're not talking here about traveling to Africa or to your local zoo to find a big, gray hippopotamus wallowing in the mud. I'm talking about an altogether different kind of HIPO—one who will make your business boom!

A HIPO is a person with HI-gh PO-tential.

Always aim to recruit people with high potential who can duplicate what you are doing. They may not be as good as you are now, but they all draw attention to themselves with their potential.

Recognizing the HIPO

Where do you find the HIPO?

HIPOs are everywhere. Look for people who:

- Are busy and active in clubs and the community
- Volunteer for local committees
- Have an entrepreneurial spirit that says "I want to give it a go"
- Love your product. They're already a great ambassador for it
- Have spare time, now that their children are at school
- Are just starting out, newly married, saving for their first home
- Enjoy the luxuries of life, company cars, and company-paid trips
- Want to pay off their credit cards and have some guilt-free spending money
- Dislike or feel bored with their current job
- Are out of work or have a spouse looking for work

- Are facing large expenses in the future, such as school and university fees, even retirement
- Are good at what they do. Chances are they will make a success of network marketing, too
- Have relinquished a full-time career to care for a young family

HIPOs are a fabulous foundation on which to build your business. As you help them develop their potential, you'll also be developing yours.

When selecting HIPOs, don't prejudge. What if someone had thought you couldn't do it before you were even asked? Many people don't show their true potential at first. Countless times I have seen people respond dramatically to the opportunity, the training, the support, and the encouragement given in network marketing. I have seen them grow and develop far beyond not only their sponsor's and family's expectations, but what's more interesting, beyond their own.

Conversely, don't let overenthusiasm tempt you to convince someone to join the business who should really remain a customer. Make sure it's what they want, not what you want for them. Be wary of pushing for recruitment quotas, promotional targets, or contests. Bring the wrong people in and you will end up with headaches, heartaches, and a lot of time spent nonproductively. Don't forget you are recruiting people, not numbers. Don't panic, take your time. There are HIPOs out there, just waiting for you to find them and give them the opportunity.

Managing Your HIPOs

Typically your downline will include many different types of distributors—wholesale buyers, retailers, minor and major players. Don't expect them all to shine through as HIPOs; your business will thrive on the variety. Be aware of the following:

- It will soon become obvious who your HIPOs are if you regularly review the performance of each member of your downline and pay full attention to everyone on an individual basis.
- Mentor your HIPOs closely for the critical first three to four months.

- Keep your herd of HIPOs to a manageable level at any one time, so you can give them the care and attention they need.
- Make sure they are as committed to their business as you are.
- Set high expectations.
- Make sure you work with those who demonstrate results, not just talk about them. You cannot afford to carry those who are not prepared, or able, to work for results.
- Offer positive, honest feedback.
- Recognize and celebrate every achievement along the way.
- Know when to step back and let a HIPO soar to full potential.

And don't neglect to approach people you admire. This may take a bit of courage, but the role of a leader in any organization is to find and develop people who have great potential. After all, if you build a business of people who don't grow, you will have a business of small people. Compare that with a business of giants, a business of HIPOs.

Don't Slow Down

Never forget that your network marketing business is just that—your own business. You own it. You are in control of it. The only person over whom you have total control is yourself. Never rely on one person, no matter how brilliant that person is. What if they cause you to relax, drop the ball, and stop recruiting new people? What will you do when, for whatever reason, they perform the vanishing act and leave? Never forget that the tide goes out as fast as it comes in.

Work hard to have as many strong people in your business as possible. It's tempting to slow down or relax your efforts when you have a winner in your downline. Reality is, they can make you vulnerable. You have to work even harder to balance them out. Enjoy them, but don't slow your pace, because it can be hard to rebuild momentum once you have slowed down. In fact, the excitement a winner generates can be a great recruiting tool. Success is a powerful magnet.

Work on the premise that the more productive the people in your business are, the healthier it will be. Quality is always better than quantity. And when you have a high quantity of high quality, you're well on your way to making your first million.

An Action Plan for New Recruits

Whenever a new recruit signs the company's agreement and joins your downline, contact them as soon as possible—the next day, or no later than the following day. Be warm, supportive and enthusiastic about their prospects for making a success of the business. Positively reinforce their decision. Make them feel welcome.

Book them in immediately for training. Encourage them to bring a friend to the training (to recruit). You can be sure they have already told their best friends what they're doing. The sooner your new recruits start recruiting, the longer the unique momentum of their early enthusiasm will last.

Get commitment from your new recruits, so they know what you expect. This means a goal and a deadline. For example, a minimum order so that you can place it with them, and at least 10 bookings in the first month. Stay in close contact. "When are you going to work on those 10 bookings? Tuesday? I'll call you Wednesday morning to see how it went." We all respond to incentives, so offer a small reward for achieving the target.

CHAPTER 17

Your Magic Network Marketing Business Tool

In network marketing, your day planner is your business. A day planner full of bookings is fundamental to your success. The more appointments you have in it, the better business you have. No one ever leaves this business with a full day planner.

Your Day Planner and Its Use

Your day planner is the most important tool you will use in your business. Not only should you discipline yourself to always have your day planner with you, it's essential to have only one day planner and one system.

If you ever do get caught without it, write the details of a contact or an appointment immediately on anything that's handy—the back of a business card or a scrap of paper. As soon as you can, transfer the details into your day planner.

Add a note to remind yourself about the person. "Bubbly brunet at the checkout." If you have made an appointment without your day planner in front of you (at a social event, for example), phone back as soon as you can, or send a note to let your prospect know the appointment is confirmed.

When you're making an appointment, the tried-and-true technique of asking, "Which will be better for you, Monday evening or Saturday morning?" works well. It brings the appointment to life in the person's mind and moves the question from "Shall I make an appointment?" to "Which day shall I make it for?" You've successfully taken them from *if* to *when*.

If you get a response such as "I'm not sure if I'm free at those times," take the initiative and say "Let's pencil it in for next Monday at 7. Here's my card. If you find you have another commitment, give me a call so we can set another date."

Your prospect knows that if they call back, you will be expecting to set another date. Always be open and direct about your intentions.

If you're working with a hostess who is hesitating about committing to a Party Plan booking, explain to her, "My day planner gets very full, very quickly, so let's go ahead and pencil in a date. I don't want you to miss out on the special hostess promotion we have this month." She'll have a better chance of a full house if she is excited about her show and has a specific date in place. Don't let her try to coordinate all the potential guests and find one date that suits them all. It's an almost impossible task. Encourage her to hold another show at a later date or take outside orders from those who can't make the date you've both settled on.

Keeping Track of It All

Whether you're working the business part-time or full-time, you're not going to be open all hours. You're a busy person with other commitments. Mark your other commitments in your day planner as well—family, friends, sports, whatever. Then, systematically mark out the times you have available for business appointments. The more clearly you identify these times, the better. I have found marking available time slots with a brightly colored highlighter or stick-on labels to be very effective. You can even color-code times for different activities—your own shows, starter shows for new recruits, and recruiting interviews.

This is a powerful method and I highly recommend it. It helps in three ways:

First, if you're working Party Plan, you can leave your day planner open in a prominent place and invite people to fill in their own appointments. Ask them to choose their own time for a show, and reserve it by clearly writing their name, address, and phone number into one of the highlighted sections. You'll find the busier your day planner looks, the more likely you are to attract bookings. We tend to equate being busy with being better, which is why everyone seems to crowd a busy restaurant while the quiet one next door stays empty.

Second, when you're booking an appointment on the telephone, it's faster, easier, and more efficient to flick through your day planner and find the slots that are highlighted but not yet allocated for an appointment.

And third, each time you open the day planner you'll be motivated to get appointments and bookings for the empty dates and times you have allocated to your business.

Postponements and Cancellations

One thing you'll learn very quickly when you have a day planner full of appointments is some get postponed and cancelled. Be prepared for this and don't be disappointed by it. Cancellations are as inevitable as night and day. If you expect them, they won't upset you. The trick is to try to save a cancellation by turning it into a postponement.

To minimize postponements and cancellations:

- Send a brief note as soon as possible to confirm the appointment and how much you are looking forward to seeing the person. It's always a pleasant surprise to find a handwritten note or card in your mailbox.
- Offer to bring muffins or donuts for morning/afternoon coffee to emphasize that you are looking forward to the meeting. This also makes things easy for your prospect.
- Use a teaser. For example, "My company is running a special promotion. Everyone I see this week will receive a small gift (a product sample, discount voucher, or other giveaway)." When you're starting out, you could use, "I have 10 gifts to give away to my first 10 bookings. I'd love you to have one."
- Include company leaflets and brochures so your prospect can appreciate what you're offering. If you've booked a show, include invitations to send to each prospective guest.

Airlines and hotels are notorious for overbooking. The reason is simple. Business experience has taught them there will be a certain percentage of no-shows (as they are known in the travel industry) who book but, for a variety of reasons, do not turn up.

I'm not recommending you book two meetings at the same time and hope that one won't happen. Rather, have a contingency plan in place. A cancellation can be a bonus if you have a backup plan—a list of calls to make, appointments to book, follow-ups to be done, confirmation notes to send out, thank-you notes to be written and posted.

You get a glorious feeling of control when you find yourself transferring a postponed appointment onto a waiting list or rebooking weeks in advance because business is so good that your day planner is already full.

Schedule Family Time, Too

When you're working your day planner, remember to slot in family time. Success in business at the expense of your family is scant success indeed. In fact, the flexibility that allows you to spend time with your family is one of the great joys of network marketing. It's what attracted me in the first place.

Like so many other network marketers, I saw it would it fit with my family life, and I could also involve my family in it.

My son David, at the age of three, could identify all the different products and enjoyed helping me organize them for packing into customer orders.

At five, my daughter Nikki was a budding makeup artist, experimenting with my tubes and testers.

My children helped me fold letters, sort orders, seal envelopes, and stick on stamps. Just as they contributed to the growth of my business, so did they sometimes make sacrifices as I worked. But they received quality education and shared new family cars, overseas vacations, and the addition of a swimming pool to our home, each of which was a goal on our family Goals List.

My children, in working with me, were also given a role model of taking responsibility for their own futures, never giving up, "Being prepared to take the bumps," as my daughter once put it.

Very few industries offer the equality of opportunity offered in network marketing. Take a look at who comes through the arrivals door first at an airport. Even today it's still mostly men who have been flying first class. But in network marketing many women are earning $100,000, $200,000, and more annually. And they're doing it in a way that allows them to have balance in their family lives.

Cherish that balance throughout your growing success, by keeping your day planner clear for family time.

Where Did the Day Go?

Imagine a typical morning. You're up early with a list of calls to make. You get the family out of the house and tell yourself you deserve a five-minute coffee break before you start. Maybe time to check the morning paper, so you know what's going on in the world. When getting the cream for coffee you realize the refrigerator needs cleaning.

You clean the refrigerator quickly, thinking about the calls you're planning to make, but because the refrigerator now looks empty you make a shopping list and head for the supermarket.

At the supermarket you meet a friend who invites you for coffee. "Well, just a quick one," you say, thinking about the calls you have to make. You know it's good to catch up with friends, maybe even talk about your business, get a few leads . . .

Imagine if, when you get home, your sister drops in to say hello, bringing her two young children. She knows you're working from home and feels you would probably enjoy some company!

Where did the day go?

Don't let your day get swallowed up. When you finally do get to the phone, don't waste precious time on unproductive chat. You are in business. Discipline yourself to be businesslike. Make writing up and adhering to your day planner a daily habit.

PART FIVE

Going for

Your Goals

CHAPTER 18

Who Wants to Be a Millionaire?

To most, the dream of being a millionaire is just that—a dream. With fingers crossed, we avidly watch the high-stake television game shows in the hope of seeing a contestant make it to the money.

Some people dream bigger dreams and try to get on one of the shows as a contestant, with the occasional big-time winner taking home the top prize. Thousands of hopeful young women helped create television game show history when they put themselves forward for a chance to marry a multimillionaire.

Still others rely on Lady Luck, whether it's a tiny flutter with a weekly lottery ticket or more desperate chances taken on the spin of the wheel or a card hand in a casino. In the United States over $50 billion a year is gambled, more than is spent on movies, videos, theme parks, and musical entertainment combined. The winners are few.

Then there are those who leave nothing to chance and take the more sure way to financial success: setting goals and developing strategies to achieve them.

Learning to run your own business is an exciting, enjoyable, and more likely way to become a millionaire. It gives you a great feeling of satisfaction and independence, as well as stimulating your personal development.

However, to achieve financial success in network marketing, as in any business, you have to master two disciplines—goal setting and time management. In this chapter we will take up the first discipline.

Goal Setting

What's so important about setting goals? For starters, you have to know *why* you're in business. In simple terms, this is goal setting.

Goal setting focuses your mind on what you will achieve. All successful people set goals, and the clearer the goals, the stronger the motivation to achieve them and the better the results.

Ask yourself, "Why am I doing this?" *Why?* is a much sharper and more compelling motivation than *How? Why?* is more than a goal, it defines the real purpose of what you're doing.

Too many people focus on *How* at the expense of *Why*, without understanding that if we have a strong enough reason *why* we're doing something, we will move a mountain. Think about the incredible voluntary fundraising efforts that happen in your community. And the impact of minority groups who collect hundreds of thousands of signatures to lobby governments with petitions.

It's been said that people work for money but will die for a cause. When people understand *Why*, their drive is stronger, and powerful results can be achieved.

Take a moment or two to think openly and honestly why you are in network marketing. Why were you first attracted to this opportunity? What do you hope to achieve from it? When you start to earn excellent money from your business, what will you do with it?

You might overhear a simple truth when you listen to young children at play, asking each other, "What do you want to be when you grow up?" In their delightful naiveté they never express it in terms of money but simply as the lifestyle they want to live.

What you want to be will become your first goal, your long-term vision for your business. For example, "I want to be a millionaire and enjoy the freedom and choice that will bring" or, more simply, "I want a better lifestyle for my family, working for myself and enjoying what I do."

Believe It

Ninety percent of all the messages we receive, we get from ourselves. It's called self-talk. Self-talk is the tape you play inside your head, and the messages you give yourself are incredibly powerful.

Henry Ford is quoted as saying, "If you think you can or you think you can't, you are probably right."

We have to constantly tell ourselves what we want to achieve in life and that we can achieve it.

When New Zealand, a country whose population is smaller than many U.S. cities, achieved its first world championship in athletics at the 1998 World Games in Athens, Greece, the whole nation cheered. It happened when athlete Beatrice Faumuina won a gold medal in the discus event.

To become world champion, all Beatrice had to do was throw the discus further than anyone else did. But as we all know, it's not quite that simple. It was reported that Beatrice took to Athens a small book of inspirational quotations from former Olympic champions. One in particular she copied in bold print and pinned on her Athens bedroom wall. It read, *"The difference between winning and losing is simply . . . belief."*

The chances of Beatrice winning didn't look good when she fouled the first, then the second of only three attempts in the qualifying round. But Beatrice believed she could throw the discus further than anyone else once, so on her third and final attempt to qualify, she unleashed a mighty 64-meter throw.

Unbelievably, this drama was repeated two nights later, in the finals.

In her first attempt, Beatrice overbalanced out of the circle and her attempt was declared a "no-throw."

Her second throw was solid, well over 63 meters. But her elation turned to horror as she saw the red flag go up, signaling another foul as the judge called that her foot had touched the circle.

Briefly she thought about challenging the call, but decided not to.

Perhaps Rudyard Kipling's poem "If" came to mind. *"If you can keep your head while all about you / Are losing theirs . . . / Yours is the earth and everything in it."*

Beatrice kept her cool, kept her focus, kept her belief in herself and re-entered the throwing circle for her one last chance at the championship. Thinking of that hand-written sign she had pinned to her bedroom wall, *"The difference between winning and losing is simply . . . belief"* she calmly went through her preliminary routine, turned, then made a huge throw that soared well past the 65-meters mark.

The indicator board flashed 66.82 meters, and the gold medal and world championship were hers. Beatrice's unquestioning belief in herself and her vision that she could, and would, win the gold medal won through.

Not everyone wants to be a world sports champion. But the same principles apply to achieving success in business. Never say, "I'll try," because "I'll try" really means you doubt your ability. Always say, "I will do it." Replace the words "I think I can" with "I know I can."

All success starts with having a crystal clear vision of where we want to be and an unshakable belief that we can get there.

Share Your Vision

There are times when we must alter the strategies we employ to reach our goals, but our vision should never alter nor falter.

When our vision falters, whatever the cause, our strength collapses, and the resulting effect on our business can be catastrophic.

One of the keys to successfully reaching your goals is sharing them. Ignore the advice of those who say keep your goals to yourself. Why would you? Because you're afraid they won't come true? Or worried about what people may think?

When I decided to put my years of network marketing experience together into this book, I shared my thoughts with my husband Wayne in a moment of enthusiasm. Not only was he immediately so supportive that I felt I had to do it, he joined me in the project. And when we spoke to friends, their high level of belief in us spurred us on.

Be prepared to put yourself on the line. Nothing demonstrates your commitment to others, and more importantly, to yourself.

The Critical Path

Make your goals specific. *What*, *Why*, and *When*. A goal without a deadline isn't a goal, it's a dream. The world is full of dreamers. The ones who succeed are those who dream in the daytime, with their eyes open and focused on a deadline.

By specifying *When* you can work backward to determine the steps and timing. This is what the experts call a Critical Path.

Because you've clearly thought through the *Why* and been specific about the *What* and *When*, you can work out the strategies, or *How* you will achieve your goal.

Break your big goal into a number of smaller goals. These become the step-by-step route toward your ultimate target. Call them strategies, if you will.

For example, if your goal is to make a million dollars, you know that can only be achieved through successfully recruiting and developing others to follow your example. Your goal within a goal then becomes "to recruit someone who, by the end of the year, achieves (*a target based on your company's remuneration plan*)."

Then work out each of the steps, or strategies, required to achieve it. If that person is not already in your team, your strategies may include: "to meet more people" by ". . . doing 10 presentations every week," which you could achieve by ". . . talking to everyone I meet about making an appointment until I fill my day planner."

Make sure each small goal contributes to your ultimate goal, or the reason you started your own business (for example, "to be earning over $100,000 annually and driving a company car within three years"), and has a clear strategy to support it.

Dream big dreams, but don't let ambitious goals obscure the smaller ones that will make things happen. It's what you do today that determines your future, not what you intend to do tomorrow. There's no point in dreaming big dreams if you're not prepared to do what it takes on a daily basis to make them come true.

It's important to aim high in achieving these smaller goals, so that you don't falter. For example, most network marketing companies offer exciting promotions and incentives for their high flyers. If your company has a six-months promotion to achieve an overseas trip, plan to achieve your target in five months to allow for unexpected events. Aiming for the bare minimum is stressful, as it leaves no room for the unforeseen and will lead to disappointment and frustration. Exceeding the goal in either time or volume brings its own satisfaction.

Visualize Your Goals

Make sure you can see yourself living your goals. Write them down and put them on the fridge door. And while you're doing that, strengthen them with a photo of your future company car or future overseas trip. Or, paste them into the front of your day planner as a daily reminder of why you're in this business. Each day, when you see pictures of the lifestyle you know you can achieve, the things you can do and can have, your goals will remain vivid and focused in your mind. Behave as if you know you cannot fail and you will move with calm confidence and assurance toward achieving your goals.

If, for example, your goal is to earn money to be able to afford to redecorate your living room, collect samples of the new fabrics, wallpaper, paint, and carpet, together with pictures of the furniture you want. This will bring the dream to life and make your pursuit of it even more determined.

Perhaps your goal is a company car. I challenge you to do this. Take your family down to the local dealership and explain your goal of driving that particular model (even choose the correct color). Take your camera with you and ask them to take a few photos of you and the family in and around the car. The dealer will love to do it for you. You may even develop a conversation that could lead to a chance to sell your product. Put the photos on your refrigerator door, on your bathroom mirror and in your day planner. You now have your family committed to helping you achieve your goals, too. The dream becomes real in everyone's mind.

Keep visualizing, keep focused and it will happen. I know, because I have seen hundreds of people just like you qualify for a company car in network marketing, many within months of joining the business.

Write Down Your Goals

Ambitious goals put energy and sparkle into your life. Dare to dream big dreams: *"If you shoot for the moon and miss, you'll still land among the stars."*

Use the following Goal Sheet or design your own. Write down your goals and the strategies for achieving them. This will put them sharply in focus. If it's not worth writing down, it's either not a real goal or you're not ready to make a commitment. In either case, it definitely won't happen. Remember, if you think you can, or think you can't, you're probably right.

Be sure to go through the same exercise with every new person you recruit. Start by asking them, "If you had enough money, what would you do with your life?" Go through the exercise I mentioned at the start of Chapter 2, having them picture their life five years from now. As they focus more on their goals, on what they really want in life—not just the money, but the lifestyle, the dreams they have for the future—they will focus less on the obstacles and more on making their dreams come true.

When the focus moves from *Who Wants to Be a Millionaire* to "Who Is Working Toward Becoming a Millionaire?" you'll find that goal setting is a vital first foundation.

Dreams or Goals?

Dreams are elusive. Goals are the tangible destination you know you are heading for.

You may dream of a pleasant family day at the lake. Do you sit at home wishing you were there? No! You load up the car and get the family on board.

You know what time to leave in order to arrive early enough to enjoy the day. You know which lake you want to go to and the best route to take. Along the way you know you are going in the right direction, because you're passing the signs that tell you you're halfway there, nearly there, and finally there.

Make your success through network marketing a goal, not a dream. Plan your destination and your route to get there. Then, start your journey.

My Goal Sheet

Why I am really in this business:

_____
_____
_____
_____
_____
_____
_____
_____
_____
_____
_____
_____

How will I achieve my goals?

What	When	How
/	/	
/	/	
/	/	
/	/	
/	/	
/	/	
/	/	
/	/	
/	/	
/	/	
/	/	
/	/	
/	/	
/	/	
/	/	
/	/	
/	/	

CHAPTER 19

Taking Control

You could have all the qualities that make an excellent direct seller—a focused determination to succeed, good people skills, strong listening and communication skills, and a positive outlook—but these will count for nothing without discipline. Without discipline, your desire to build a successful business will remain forever a dream.

In Chapter 18 I said that there were two disciplines that every successful network marketer must master—goal setting and time management. In other words, discipline is about setting goals, then doing what is necessary to achieve them. In this chapter we will take up the second of these two disciplines.

Time Management

Time management means refusing to be swayed by the countless distractions that can easily take over your day and destroy your progress. The things you say you are going to do won't help. You can't change the amount of time you have, but you can change how you use it. Use every minute of your available time to do the things that will help you achieve your goals.

Either you control your time or it controls you. It's that simple. Discipline is not something most of us are born with. It's a skill successful people learn. Without it, your chances of success are limited. The only people who attribute success to luck are those who don't achieve it. By contrast, any successful person will tell you, "The harder I work, the luckier I get."

Belief alone is not enough. You have to be prepared to do whatever it takes to achieve your goal and to let go of the things that won't help.

Ask yourself, "Is it written on my Goal Sheet?" If not, will it contribute? If it won't, don't let it steal time from you.

Discipline means being prepared to learn new habits. It means giving up indulgences like meandering through daily chores such as housework and shopping, spending time on long phone calls, mindless television watching, or computer games. You can't do those things and build a million-dollar business. Decide which activities and projects are priorities and say a firm "No" to the rest.

Network marketing is about reward for results. Results come from effort. The more time you put into your business, the better results you will get. That's the simple truth of it. And the upside is, the greater the results, the greater the rewards. That's when network marketing gets exciting.

Once you have written your goals and planned how to achieve them, think carefully about the time that you are prepared to invest in your business. Plan it, and then stick to it.

Your To Do List

The two most effective tools ever invented for time management are . . . pencil and paper. The tools you use to create your daily To Do list.

Every evening, write your To Do list for the following day. Consider every task you have to accomplish and list them all. The order doesn't matter.

Focus on what you have to do to reach the goals written on your Goal Sheet.

I often play a game with people I'm working with, claiming I can accurately predict their future. Most people are fascinated by the thought of being able to glimpse into the unknown, so when I have their attention and they are curious to know what I see ahead for them, I say:

"Show me what you do daily and I'll show you your future."

What you do today will determine where you are tomorrow. There's no astrology or crystal ball gazing in it.

It's what you do today that counts. And you have to make every day count.

List everything on your To Do list. Small tasks like making a dental appointment or delivering an order, and bigger tasks like approaching a potential distributor. Include all the details necessary to accomplish each task. For example, when I am compiling my list I write the phone number next to the name of each person I will be calling and the address of those to whom I'll be sending a note. This saves time, keeps me focused, and allows me to work at a good pace through my To Do list during the day. It also takes away any obstacle I might put up, such as "I couldn't find the phone number."

Write everything down, however trivial. Refer to the list constantly throughout the day. As you cross each one off and move on to the next, you'll get a rewarding sense of accomplishment.

Don't worry if sometimes you don't finish everything on your list. The busiest people I know always have a full In tray. You'll find as you work your list that you can't keep putting off until tomorrow those things that must be done today. Tomorrow has been reserved for what you have to do tomorrow. That's why I always make the last part of my day writing my To Do list for the next day. I prepare it the night before, so I'm ready for a flying start at the morning when I'm fresh and invigorated.

When you get to the end of the day and there are still things left on your list, you have already started tomorrow's list. You know what's right at the top, the number one priority. Focus on what you achieved today, not on what you didn't manage. The key question is always "Am I making tangible progress and getting results?" If so, things will be fine. Relax and enjoy the journey to your goal.

Your To Do list is your work plan for the day. Plan your work and work your plan.

Distractions Happen

Instill in yourself the discipline that your To Do list will take priority over whatever else comes along during your day. Distractions will happen, and they're okay as long as you control them. Have the courage to cut short a chatty phone call. The phone is an incredible time waster. You can close a phone call nicely: "I won't keep you, I know you're busy" or, "I must go now, I have so much to do. It was great to hear from you." If friends call at an inappropriate time, tell them, "I'm working now, may I call you back?"

Never be too busy to return calls. No matter how busy I am, I return calls promptly because I know the call will be important to the caller. My business is people and returning calls promptly tells people I have respect for them.

WHO'S DRIVING?

You won't reach your destination if you keep getting out of the driver's seat and letting someone else take control.

Learn to say "No thanks" or "Not just at the moment" to the things that will prevent you from achieving your goal. Time wasters are a big trap, and it takes self-discipline to avoid them.

You are a businessperson, running your own business. You are earning, or on your way to earning, an enviable income. Learn to delegate tasks that can easily and cheaply be handled by someone else. Enjoy the power, the exhilaration, of being in control of your time, your future, and your life.

The test is to ask yourself, "If I do this, will it help me achieve my goal?" Or, in realistic business terms, "Will doing this make money for me?"

Network marketing becomes more exciting as the momentum swells and the results start to show. Never lose that momentum. You can't afford to take a break in this business. Drop the ball and you have to start the game again. Momentum is everything.

One of the biggest disappointments I see in this business is when a successful distributor lets the little distractions build up and take over. When this happens, they begin to lose their forward momentum. Their business starts to falter and they quickly become disillusioned. A different type of momentum takes over. Growing disappointment. A feeling of failure, even anger that success is eluding them.

Invariably, they start looking around for others to blame. Downline distributors who aren't living up to expectations. An Upline not giving support. The company doing things wrongly. A product that isn't right. The fault is everywhere but within.

WHAT IF IT'S THE COMPANY'S FAULT?

Success in network marketing is 80 percent you and 20 percent the company you have chosen to work with. Your success is in your hands, no one else's. This may sound like a hard truth. It is, so believe it.

If you feel you have a genuine grievance with the company you have chosen, resolve it, accept it, or move on. Don't let yourself be dragged into a business or lifestyle of unhappiness, disappointment, and disillusionment.

You can't hide these emotions. Know when it's time to quit and join a company that better suits your needs, if that's the only answer. But be honest first, and ask yourself "'Is it really the company or is it me?"

Learn to accept everything about your company and your industry, not just the parts that especially suit you. Most network marketing companies have an enormous independent distributor base and create programs that suit the majority. Be prepared to "lose on the swings and gain on the merry-go-round."

Resist the urge to drag others down by trying to get them to support your viewpoint. Accept that no one can please all the people all the time.

WHAT IF IT'S YOU?

Don't give up if you think the problem may be you. The first step toward recovery is accepting that you own both the problem and the responsibility for fixing it. Once it's resolved, you'll be able to look back and see that every wrong attempt discarded became a step forward.

We all lose energy at times. We even lose our way sometimes. This is a good time to plug into the energy of someone who is going in the right direction. Be aware that like attracts like and resist the urge to enter the zone of negativity, or you will find yourself on a downward spiral.

I often joke that we shouldn't share our problems with those around us, because "Half don't care and the other half are glad we have them." It's a bit tongue-in-cheek, but the point is to resist the temptation to burden others with our personal grievances.

Curiously, human nature sometimes compels us to seek solace among those who share our dissatisfaction. The only thing more contagious than enthusiasm is the lack of it. Be wary of the signals you are sending out. While negatives thrive on negativity and gossips thrive on gossip, happiness attracts happiness and success attracts success.

Learn to step neatly around anyone who can bring you down. The only time these people are happy is when they see others sliding down to join them at their sorry level. Instead, surround yourself with positive people. Think back to the times you have been at your most powerful . . . it will have been when you were at your most positive.

Small Steps Get You Back on the Track

I know that sometimes, when we're feeling a bit flat, it's difficult to bounce back up again. But you must! Believe that you will be back again, and the sooner you bounce out of it, the better. The best way I know to pick yourself up is to take practical steps, however small, to make things start happening. All businesses have ups and downs and it's up to you to get the ball rolling again.

The best antidote to disappointment is action! Positive action will give you what you want. Step up what you're doing and stop focusing on what you're feeling. Focus outward, not on feeling sorry for yourself.

People not responding to you? Join Toastmasters, ITC, or a similar organization to improve your communication and leadership skills and meet new people.

Feeling drab? Treat yourself to a new hairstyle or change of color. If you can't afford a trip to the salon, purchase a home color kit and have fun experimenting. Check out your wardrobe to rediscover outfits you have forgotten, or ways of putting your clothes together in new combinations. Sometimes all it takes is a new tie to update and transform a suit.

Feeling unappreciated? Turn it around by taking the initiative. Surprise your partner or family with a special trip or treat. Visit or call a relative you have not been in contact with for a long time.

Feeling down? There are plenty of people worse off than you are. Do something for someone else, with no strings attached. Send money to a charity. Offer to babysit. Help a friend spring-clean their home. Wayne and I call it an "A-OK"—a little "Act Of Kindness" that helps us feel "A-OK," too. Sometimes it's the smallest gesture, but we try to do an A-OK every day.

Feeling gloomy? Buy pots of colorful flowers to brighten your living areas. Or give flowers to brighten someone else's day.

Not going anywhere? Perhaps you have lost focus, or you're aiming for the impossible—for example, becoming a great success in network marketing while still holding on to your full-time job, or splitting your energies over too many interests. Often it helps to take time out and read an uplifting book.

If you feel people are not responding to you as well as you wish, try playing audiotapes in your car on your way to appointments. Motivational speakers or tapes from seminars you have attended can be uplifting, and will put you into a positive, upbeat, confident frame of mind when it's needed most.

Running out of steam? Call your upline or people you admire in your organization and plug into their energy for a while. If they're achieving what you're aiming for, ask for their advice.

Feeling a little out of touch with the dot-com revolution? Sign up for a short, inexpensive course. You'll meet new people and enjoy the satisfaction of mastering a new skill.

The point is to focus on the solution, not the problem.

How we deal with challenges and setbacks shapes our character and our life. No one else can make you the person or the success you want to be. Tell yourself, "If it's going to be, it's up to me!"

We may not be able to control events, but we can control how we respond to them. It's not what happens to us that's significant, it's how we react to those events. And that's the part we have control over.

Motivating Others

We all have incredible power over the emotions of those around us. Notice how if one morning there's a grouch in your house, the whole house feels it. Yet, it's hard to feel down when you walk outside and there's a big, bright blue sky filled with warm sunshine.

Imagine taking a plane journey when take-off is on a gray and gloomy rain-filled day. Before long, the plane climbs above the clouds, which are white and fluffy on top, and you're flying through a bright sunny sky. As leaders, it's our job to be on top, to be the sunshine, despite any gloom below.

I know this is easily said. How do you achieve it? You create your own vision, your own totally non-negotiable belief in yourself and your ability to make your vision a reality. When you are confident about where you are going and how you will get there, your confidence will radiate out to other people and strengthen their personal belief, too.

Become confident in where you are going and not only will the path become clearer and the obstacles easier to overcome, you'll find others motivated to take the journey with you.

People who seem to have more than their fair share of lucky breaks get them because others are attracted to the energy and enthusiasm that come with success. You can't fake those emotions, but when success brings them genuinely, they are incredibly contagious.

Motivation clarifies our priorities, and priorities and results are inseparable.

As a leader, you have the power to fuel or extinguish the flame of motivation, by how you keep the vision alive.

Bringing Your Vision to Life

Vision is the ability to see a situation as it is, then plan how you want it to be. Without it, there is no direction, no motivation.

When I visited the statue of David in Italy I was spellbound by Michelangelo's artistic vision. The statue is so lifelike you can almost see blood pulsing through the arteries running down David's arm.

Michelangelo had a vision of how he wanted the statue to be. So, chip by chip, he cut away the pieces of stone he didn't need to reveal the perfection within. The result was a work of beauty that has awed millions.

We all have special qualities that can be exposed if we have the vision and courage to chip away at the blocks and reveal them.

It's so much easier to find success if we have the courage to tackle both the advances and the setbacks in our lives.

When you have your life planned, managed, and under control, you'll find you are relaxed and happy. And it's relaxed and happy people who are the most successful, because they're also best in attracting others who want to be like them and share their clear vision and success.

Are You Getting Things Done?

Some people thrive on having a head full of pressures and deadlines. They rush through the day trying to achieve, in no particular priority, all the things their head is bursting with. At the end of the day, they have a sense of having done a good day's work—until two o'clock the next morning when they suddenly sit bolt upright in bed, having remembered something important that slipped their mind during the day.

Paradoxically, sometimes when they do write their To Do list, the brain somehow thinks the things written down have been done, because they've been taken out of the mind's *urgent* file.

If this is you, discipline yourself to write your To Do list, and refer to it throughout the day. As you feel a small buzz of satisfaction from crossing off each task you complete, you'll soon start to appreciate the value of time management.

If you're an existing network marketer, you already know about goal setting and managing your time effectively. You probably also know that to keep advancing and elevating yourself, you must keep improving your techniques and skills. And that means a little self-evaluation from time to time.

The following quick self-evaluation chart will help you focus on how you're spending your time and plan how to improve. There are no right answers. Just answer honestly to get the proper picture of your present and potential performance!

You will see that most of the activities involve face-to-face contact with others. There's a good reason for this. The more time you spend face-to-face, the quicker your business will grow and the more quickly you'll make your first network marketing million. Network marketing is a relationship business and you won't build enough relationships unless you're out there meeting people, talking face-to-face.

Activities like planning, bookkeeping, and creating a database on your PC are all extras. They won't contribute to your million-dollar income, so be wary of falling into the administration trap. It's very easy to keep yourself busy *being* busy. The only busyness that works is meeting people, making sales, and duplicating your efforts through recruiting, training, and leading productive leaders.

Personal Productivity Self-Test

Completing this simple chart will allow you to check your productivity and then develop strategies for putting your focus where you will make more income.

My Activity Analysis
(percentage of time spent)

Activity	What I do	What I wish I did
Making Bookings	%	%
Recruitment Interviews	%	%
Party Plan Selling	%	%
One-on-one Selling	%	%
Telephone Servicing	%	%
Face-to-Face Servicing	%	%
Training/Group Meetings	%	%
Telephoning Downline	%	%
Mentoring HIPOs	%	%
Ordering/Deliveries	%	%
Administration/Bookwork	%	%

CHAPTER 20

Keeping an Eye on Business

Although office work won't directly make you more money, efficiency will make life a lot easier for you. As your business grows, being businesslike will help you become more effective. It will free your valuable time, allowing you to achieve the goals you have set. Early in your business development, prepare yourself to handle your future growth. Isolate an area, preferably a room in your home, to establish your office. Just one corner in a room is fine. Countless successful businesses have been set up and run from the kitchen table.

The Essentials

You don't need everything at once. Gradually work toward assembling the essentials:

- First priority is a separate bank account for your business transactions.
- Telephone with voice mail, caller ID, call forwarding, and outgoing message facilities. If you have teenagers in the home, a separate, dedicated telephone line for your business is essential! Similarly, if your family has an Internet connection using the home phone line, you'll need a separate, dedicated business line.
- Cell phone.
- Day planner.
- Demonstration product and literature.
- Customer Filing system. A simple card index will suffice at the beginning, but sooner or later a computer will make life a lot easier.

- Stationery supplies.
- White or clear adhesive labels to affix to products—"To reorder, please call (*your name, your phone number*)."
- Business cards and personalized notepaper.
- Self-inking stamp with your name and phone number, to print on all your literature.
- Business supplies, including petty cash vouchers.
- Street directory.
- Calculator.
- Your Opportunity Kit.
- Accounting/tax record book or program.
- Mileage logbook for your vehicle.
- Filing drawer or cabinet.

When you can afford them (from your first paychecks):

- Fax machine.
- Copier.
- Computer.
- Television and VCR.
- DVD player, if your company utilizes DVD.

TAKE CREDIT

Another essential is to make it as easy for your customers to pay you as possible. As soon as possible organize a credit card merchant facility. This guarantees your payment at the time of order and allows you to deliver more quickly. Although you will pay a small percentage of each sale to the credit card company, you will have the advantage of guaranteed payment when you take an order. You will be able to accept payment for phone, Internet, and mail orders and save yourself the time and trouble of frequent visits to the bank.

LOOK GOOD IN PRINT

A local printer will help with your business card and letterhead. Your company probably has a template and style guide to follow. If not, choose a paper stock and color that suit your personality. Make sure they're going to be easy to read. Include your name, company, address, phone, fax, and e-mail details. Choose a typeface that is simple and looks professional. Avoid fancy typefaces that quickly become dated and are often difficult to read. Keep it simple. Your letterhead and business card are "you" so be sure they present your best possible image. If you have a home computer, you may be able to set up your own letterhead.

Office Work Is Part of Your Job

Set aside time each day for the office. Keep files and records up to date. Read and respond to correspondence, especially from your company. (I have often seen an otherwise effective leader miss out on a deadline or promotional event by not keeping up with reading company correspondence.) Review the sales figures of your downline and follow-up where necessary. Maintain your books.

Remember to keep every receipt for purchases from the first day, to pass to your accountant at tax filing time. Note on every receipt the date, location, and reason for the expense.

The easier you make life for your accountant, the less you will be charged in fees!

As an independent, self-employed businessperson, you have the same financial responsibilities as any businessperson or corporation. Taking care of business means keeping accurate business records. Why? First, because record keeping is a legal requirement. Second, because without proper records you can't run your business efficiently. And third, you have an ethical responsibility to run your business within the guidelines of sound business practice.

Business records:

- Reflect the true state and health of your business
- Help you identify and address areas of strength and weakness
- Allow you to make profitable decisions
- Ensure you pay the correct amount of tax, no more and no less

You have a responsibility to yourself and your business to keep accurate, up-to-date records. This is the area where many people with a small business fall down.

Keeping Accurate and Complete Records

Incomplete accounting causes grief when the tax department comes calling, as they will. Without proper records you have no real understanding of your earnings, and therefore no idea how much money you have available for saving, spending, or reinvesting in your business.

How do you keep your records? Simple is best! You'll require a few basic tools:

- Your day planner—it's your record of appointments, bookings, entertainment, interviews, mileage and travel, deliveries, training, and even customer phone numbers. Never throw away a finished day planner. You may be required to produce it to support expense claims, even after many years.
- A standard columned accounting book, where you record all transactions:

INCOME

Date	Amount	Taxes	Who From	Source of income

EXPENSES

Date	Amount	Taxes	Who To	Reason for expense

Your expenses can then be defined under a variety of headings, for example: Demonstration Product, Gifts, Vehicle, Home Office, Stationery, Display Materials, Promotions, Bank Charges, Drawings, Other (such as magazine subscriptions, entertainment, postage).

Balance your books monthly, filing all:

- Payment records and statements from your company
- Bank statements, check stubs, credit card statements
- Receipts for large amounts that will relate to check, direct debit, or credit card payments
- Receipts for smaller cash amounts, such as coffee you bought for an interview, parking, gift-wrap, postage.

Incidentals can add up to a sizable amount, so balance them monthly, reimburse yourself monthly, and record in your book. It's a good idea to place all miscellaneous receipts into an envelope and write the total on the front with the date and details of your reimbursement.

Tax Deductions

You will be surprised at what you can claim in the way of deductible expenses. In general, the principle applies that if the expense was incurred in the process of helping you make money, then it could be considered deductible. Different jurisdictions have different rules, so always get qualified professional accounting and tax advice. Expenses that may be judged as tax deductible, provided you can prove they relate directly and solely to your business, include:

- Training and seminar costs, including travel, meals, and accommodation if necessary
- Publications, books, and tapes relating to your business
- Share of house expenses such as mortgage interest, rental costs, city taxes, utilities, housekeeping, insurance, maintenance, and depreciation, if you have an office or designated place in your home from which your business is run
- Products you use in demonstrations, testing, and for gifts
- Vehicle expenses
- Stationery, postage, and courier expenses
- Entertainment costs
- Display and promotional expenses
- Telephone and Internet fees

- Child minding
- Other miscellaneous costs

Collate everything in a binder and keep up to date. Get into the routine of writing your records while the transaction is still fresh in your mind, rather than putting it off until later.

By keeping accurate records you are developing invaluable skills and running your business professionally. Keep records from the day you start and you'll be building a healthy, stress-free business, run on sound business practices.

GET EXPERT ADVICE

Get good accounting advice. Find a tax expert who understands the direct selling industry. Your upline or other distributors may be able to make recommendations.

Professional advice is tax deductible, and the right expertise will save, rather than cost you money.

You will be amazed at how much your accountant or tax advisor can help. They will show you how to improve your records and structure your business to maximize your profits and minimize your tax.

The IRS has the ability (both general and specific) to help. I recommend you call your local Government office or tax department for copies of any literature and booklets they have with guidelines for direct selling or small businesses.

Don't Forget Your Priorities

Remember always that people drive this business, not paperwork. Don't get caught up in administration at the expense of getting out there among people. Schedule office time into your day planner and do the paperwork—ordering, filing, correspondence, bookkeeping, and so on—at a regular, planned time. The best measure of your future success will always be the amount of time you spend with people, growing your business.

Avoiding the Cash Traps

Many businesses fail not through lack of sales growth but through mismanagement of cash. Make a commitment to the health of your business by avoiding these cash traps:

- Don't ever buy inventory to achieve a payment level or promotion target. A small amount of inventory to fulfill urgent or repeat orders of your most popular items is okay, but anything more is a sign you are heading for trouble. Discourage your downline from this practice also.
- Don't mingle your personal and your business bank accounts. Always keep them separate.
- Don't spend customers' money. It's tempting to take a few dollars for coffee or groceries, but don't. This will lead you to cash flow problems when it comes to pay the company. Even a little, taken occasionally, adds up very quickly. Customers' money belongs to your business, not to you.
- Pay all monies into your business account and draw your income from that account. Always see your business as a separate entity in your head and in practice.
- Don't get into debt. Only buy what you have cash for and don't make a purchase in anticipation of a commission check. Interest rates are exorbitant, as are penalty charges for dishonored and late payments. Always keep a positive cash flow.
- Don't spend more than you can afford on gifts and giveaway product. The sooner you make a profit the better, so use company offers and incentives fully, trying not to add additional incentives. Let the quality and value of your product do the selling, not bribes and gifts.
- Don't do your own tax return. The cost of paying a tax specialist will be more than repaid when dealing with the IRS.

CHAPTER 21

Turn on to Technology

Technology is revolutionizing our industry. It brings you a whole new world of communication tools to help you run your business faster, more effectively, and more profitably. You won't want, and can't afford, to ignore these ongoing changes. Technology will play a fundamental role in the future of network marketing, not replacing but enhancing our industry. It gives you unlimited potential to manage spectacular growth, while continuing to keep your overhead to a minimum.

If you're one of those people who suffer from techno-fear, you could be locked out of amazing opportunities. The only way to overcome fear is knowledge. Learn to use these new tools and keep up to date with them. They provide powerful ways to improve your business and enable you to communicate more often and more effectively with your customers, your downline, and your company.

Let's look at some of the technologies that have the power to make a dramatic impact on your business.

Personal Computers

Your Personal Computer makes it easy for you to be as fast and efficient working from home as the largest companies. Or even more so.

We live in an increasingly computer-driven world. And anyone who ignores the dot-com explosion will feel increasingly alienated from the new way of doing things.

A PC can help you manage your database of customers and downline distributors, record expenses, generate professional letters, and send personalized correspondence at the touch of a button.

Your computer, when linked to your company through the Internet, will facilitate an amazing flow of information. You can check your personal

138

volume and your rewards and rebates, keep track of personal and downline sales, download reports, and receive and send inquiries and information.

You'll also use your PC to produce address lists, newsletters, correspondence, envelopes, and labels. It will enable you to improve your customer servicing by planning your call cycles and sorting your customers into purchase cycles or product groupings.

While it will never replace your personal input (that will always be a unique strength of network marketing), your PC will allow you to automate your business, dramatically increasing the time you will be able to spend on face-to-face contact. And computers are becoming less expensive and more user-friendly every year.

If your household doesn't have a PC—no problem! Within your neighborhood there will be a computer bureau or secretarial service that will do it for you at minimal cost, saving you an enormous amount of time. You may even find an opportunity to develop another customer or downline recruit, as they see firsthand how well your business is going.

If you're committed to making a big success of the business, I recommend making the purchase of a computer a priority investment as soon as your business begins to grow. You'll find it's a relatively small investment, including paying for training, which will be quickly repaid through increased efficiency and productivity.

Fax Machines

It's no longer quite high-tech, but a fax machine is still a quick and simple way to communicate a consistent and immediate message to all members of your downline. A simple one-page message with news, training tips, and recognition can be circulated instantly. Modern fax machines can be programmed to send the same message to a group of different phone numbers at the push of one button. Customer orders can be faxed into your home, and information can be sent to you immediately from the company, your upline, and your downline. Multipurpose machines can also function as a fax, copier, and computer printer. Alternatively, your computer can be programmed to send and receive faxes, saving the additional expense of a separate machine.

Copiers

If you intend copying newsletters, memos, order forms, and other documents in large numbers, a high-speed copier will more than repay your investment. Until you can afford one, use your local neighborhood copying service.

Telephone Technologies

CELL PHONES

Love them or hate them, cell phones are now an integral part of our everyday life. You are going to be spending most of your time away from your home phone and a cell phone will allow you to run your business from wherever you are, rather than being tied to your home office. Make sure you organize call-forwarding from your home to your cell phone.

VOICE MAIL

A voice-mail facility on both your home and cell phone, will ensure you don't miss the calls which generate your income.

OUTBOUND VOICE MAIL

This service is perfect for busy network marketing leaders, allowing you to record a voice message and transmit it simultaneously to many phone numbers. Provided your downline distributors subscribe to an answering service (which you recommend they do), the message will be recorded instantly on their voice mail. You can use the service any time, day or night, without disturbing the receiver. Successful network marketing leaders who use it on a regular basis send:

- Inspirational thoughts and training tips
- Up-to-the-minute news
- Progress reports and recognition of achievements
- Updates on forthcoming events, new product releases, and promotional news
- Welcomes to and introductions for new people in your downline.

As you develop your business you will be involved in company events and training for which not all your downline will be eligible. After each event, you can easily spend a few minutes recording a message to share what you learned. The system is easy, economical, and time effective. It's just another part of the technology revolution that is making network marketing more efficient and more dynamic for everyone.

THREE-WAY CALLING

Improve your business even more by installing a three-way calling facility on your telephone. It will enable your newer downline recruits to link their prospect to you in a three-way call, listening and learning while you talk directly to their prospect.

INFORMATION HOTLINE

Arranging a toll-free number will allow your downline and your customers unlimited access to product and promotional information and an easy ordering facility, when you're not available. Your business is effectively open 24 hours a day!

TELECONFERENCING

Imagine inviting an unlimited number of people to call from the comfort of their own home or office, at a prearranged time, and listen in to a "live" presentation over the telephone. More than an exciting, dramatic, and convenient way of sharing news, teleconferencing can be used to expose your people and prospects to the best dynamic company personnel, motivational speakers, and special events.

VIDEO-CONFERENCING

Video-conferencing takes teleconferencing a step further, broadcasting your image, or that of anyone in your organization, live anywhere across the country or across the world. It's a brilliant way to share excitement, recognition, inspiration, and education with as many people as possible. You don't need to be left behind if your company doesn't have this facility, as VHS copies of conferences can also be couriered and watched at home anytime.

The Internet

The Internet is already being used by hundreds of thousands of companies around the world. Network marketing industry leaders, including Amway, Nu Skin, New Vision, and Rexall are already investing millions of dollars in this technology to support their distributors. Soon every network marketing company wanting to stay in business will have an Internet presence. Your own home page, linked to the company's Web site, will allow you to take orders and share information with your customers, 24 hours a day.

In the years ahead, we will use technologies we can only dream of right now. But don't be daunted if you have not yet embraced them. However exciting these tools are, they will always be just that—tools, designed to support but not replace the fundamental factors of your business. They will never replace the power of face-to-face contact.

Personal contact is, and always will be, the special magic of network marketing. In network marketing, the stronger the personal contact, the stronger the bonds you build, and the stronger your business will be.

CHAPTER 22

Promoting Your Business

Network marketing companies invest in you, their distributor, rather than in mass-media advertising. Although advertising and publicity won't guarantee you success, there are times when you can boost your growth by investing in a little self-promotion when you feel fresh contacts are needed.

Some Self-Promotion Ideas

Here are 10 inexpensive ideas to help you tell the world more about yourself:

1. A listing in the Yellow Pages of the telephone directory
2. A simple advertisement in a local newspaper
3. A notice on a community notice board
4. An interview with your suburban newspaper
5. A minor sponsorship involvement with a local event that suits your product, for example, a bridal fair, fashion show, or charity fundraiser
6. An Internet home page, linked to your company's Web site
7. A mailbox drop of company literature, in your chosen area
8. A career survey in a high foot-traffic area (See the example at the end of this chapter.)
9. Video- or audiotapes promoting network marketing and your business
10. Booths at a shopping mall, trade show, or community fair

Booths

A booth at a mall, show, or fair can be particularly effective if you are well organized. Your initial investment may be high, but you can reduce the cost if you share with others in your downline. These venues give you the opportunity to meet a lot of people face-to-face and generate new leads to follow up.

Use this checklist when planning your booth.

- Choose a site where there will be high traffic. A corner booth or one close to the main stage, the entry or exit doors, or the restrooms will give you good visibility. Don't think you'll save money by selecting a low-rent site in a forgotten cul-de-sac.
- Music, lighting, and free samples will help draw people to your stand.
- A live demonstration will generate interest and sales, especially if you are promoting highly demonstrable products like cleaners, cookware, and cosmetics or products that can be sampled, such as foods or drinks.
- As trade shows are often held over a weekend, many people will bring children with them. A free colorful balloon or candy for the children will guarantee that people stop and chat.
- Offering a free draw for an attractive prize (perhaps a gift basket crammed with your products) will allow you to collect names and phone numbers easily for follow-up. A few days later, make calls to all the new contacts you have made.
- A special offer will help generate sales if you are selling at your booth and can easily be extended when you make your follow-up telephone call. "Because our special offer (*repeat details of the offer*) was so popular, we have decided to extend it to the end of next week."

Introduce yourself by saying something along these lines: "Hi there, Jenny. This is (*your name and your company name*). Thanks for stopping by our booth at the (*name of show*) last week. I'm calling to follow-up on the (*special offer*) we were offering as a promotion. And because our gift basket draw was so popular, we have created another draw for everyone who makes an appointment for (*your product line*) by next Friday. May I book you in? I have next Thursday at 10:00 A.M. or next Monday night at 7:00 P.M. free."

These events are a big investment in time and money. They require plenty of planning and energy, before and after the event, but they can be great fun, facilitate team building, and generate a windfall of worthwhile leads and results.

If the event is a local school fair, you can generate goodwill by helping to raise funds (donating the proceeds of a raffle for a basket of your products, for example) while promoting your business.

Videos and Audios

When it comes to promotion, often the simplest is best. Videos are an excellent recruiting tool. They give a carefully structured, professional presentation with action, sound, music, and information. Hopefully your company has a video that is so sensational you believe everyone who sees it will be impressed.

Alternatively, you may wish to purchase generic videos, which promote the advantages of network marketing as a business. Many of these are promoted through industry magazines.

Purchase five or six videos and plan to have them out working for you all the time. How do you get them out and about? Try this and see how well it works:

Call the person you want to send a video to. Allow yourself five minutes to introduce it. Get a conversation going and listen to your prospect. Identify one or two of the particular hot buttons you can push—school fees, holidays, a new appliance, a new car, overseas travel, home improvements, a chance to control their own life, a chance to break away from a nine-to-five routine.

Ask if they are willing to set aside seven to ten hours a week, working from home.

Tell them you would like to lend them the video. Explain that it runs just 10 minutes (or whatever its length). Ask if you can call them two days later so they can tell you what they thought of it.

What if you get an outright rejection? So what! It only cost you five minutes of your life. It won't depress you, because you know you're going to come up with sand more often than gold.

The conversation also gives you a good opener for another lead. And you're always looking for leads. Think positively. Instead of saying to yourself, "You're rejecting me personally," remind yourself to use every chance to ask for a referral, so you can keep sifting new sand to find the gold.

Ask, "Who else might like to see the video?"

Videos, in most people's minds, are equated with entertainment. And we all like to be entertained. The same applies if your company has audio recruiting tapes. Most people have a cassette player in their car these days and spend time driving that could be utilized listening to your tape.

When sending the tape, include a selection of company literature to read and a brief hand-written note thanking them for taking the time to view it.

How to Follow Up

When you follow up two days later, don't ask "Did you like the video?" or "Can I sign you up?" Instead, keep it in their perspective. Ask, "What did you find interesting about it?" Listen closely to their answers, as they will tell you how to take the conversation forward.

If they didn't respond well to the video, it's not because the video's wrong, it will be that the opportunity or the timing are not appropriate.

When you do get a positive response, keep talking about the video rather than directly (at this stage) asking them about changing their life and becoming part of your downline. "What was most interesting?" "What was most important?"

You'll notice these questions are positive and upbeat. Don't go searching for negatives and objections to overcome.

Learn to listen in full. Don't interrupt. Don't cut off. Don't be too keen to jump in with an answer. Often we think we know what the other person is going to say and try and finish the sentence for them, as if implying empathy. Don't!

Listen, then think about what the real question is that the prospect is asking.

Be very careful about the actual words you use in your reply. "You have a good point there, but . . ." actually sounds to the other person like, "You *don't* have a good point there."

Don't be too quick in your rebuttal with a litany of logic, facts, or figures. They've already heard the facts and figures they need in the video presentation.

Recall your early days in network marketing, when you felt nervous, apprehensive, and unsure. You are discussing what could be a major change in your prospect's lifestyle. Show empathy with them.

Once you have determined the reasons, thoughts, and concerns behind a question, try answering with a true-life success story, preferably your own. Alternatively, you could use someone else in your company whom your prospect could identify with. This is where a three-way call with someone from your upline helping out could be valuable. Or perhaps you could make a generalization that sounds believable. "A lot of people feel like that at first, but once you get started and do it a few times, you become more familiar, more comfortable and . . ."

Picture your prospect poised on the edge of making the decision. This is a very sensitive time. An attempt to push could backfire, and they could shrink back from the decision. Your role is to reassure and encourage and to do it with genuine enthusiasm for your opportunity, your products, and your potential recruit's future prospects.

A good way to keep the conversation flowing toward a decision is to follow up each of your answers with a comment like "Does that sound interesting?" or "Can you see how it can happen for you, too?" Keep listening to what they're saying and think about what's behind the words.

If you present your video or audiotapes the right way to the right people, you'll soon have new members in your team. And don't forget to ask everyone, "Who else do you know who might be interested in seeing the video? Thank you. Anyone else?"

Five-Minute Career Survey

A career survey is a creative way to maximize recruiting opportunities. Ask passers-by if they will spare five minutes to complete the questionnaire. Use or adapt the format outlined here.

Thank you for taking the time to complete this survey. Please print clearly, and check the appropriate boxes.

Name ....

Address ....

....

Daytime phone ....

Evening phone ....

Best time to call ....

	Yes	No
1. Do you enjoy your current work?	☐	☐
2. Do you earn enough money?	☐	☐
3. Does your job offer challenge and variety?	☐	☐
4. Do you have enough spare time to enjoy life?	☐	☐
5. Can you see yourself in the same job next year?	☐	☐

If you answered "No" to any of the above, or are looking for a change of career, please continue.

	Yes	No
6. Do you like working with people?	☐	☐
7. Would you like a higher income?	☐	☐
8. Would you like more free time?	☐	☐
9. Does being your own boss appeal to you?	☐	☐
10. Are you willing to work at least 10 hours per week to build your own business?	☐	☐

If you answered "Yes" to any of the above, you may be suitable for a career promoting our products. To find out more, please check one of the following:

☐ Send me an information pack.

☐ Call me to book an appointment to discuss this business opportunity.

(Add your own name and contact details to the survey form.)

A New Business Launch

The best way to start promoting your business is a simple, well-organized new business launch.

It's the perfect time to invite your hottest recruiting prospects, and other friends and family members, too.

Tell prospects something like this:

"I'm celebrating the launch of my new business and I'd like you to be there. My sponsor who introduced me to the business and is teaching me the ropes will be there and I would like you to meet her/him. There will be a short presentation on my new business, a chance to preview the products I'm now representing, and, of course, (*an outline of refreshments, drinks, nibbles, coffee, cake, or whatever is appropriate*). I am very excited about what I am now doing so please come and celebrate with me and give me the chance to show you what it's all about. Your support means a lot to me."

PART SIX

There's No

Business Like

Show Business

CHAPTER 23

It's Party Time

There are few more effective or lucrative ways to run many network marketing businesses than through Party Plan. I use the name Party Plan to cover Show Plan, workshops, group demonstrations, previews, and any other presentation to a group of people.

Party Plan is the quickest way to increase your customer base. It provides you with a rich source of people to sell to and recruit. It's the simplest way to keep your day planner full of bookings and, without doubt, it's the most effective way to train the people you sponsor.

Not all products are suited to shows, but most are.

Party Plan is the method of showcasing your product line to more than one person at a time. Talking to five people at once is clearly more efficient that saying the same thing five times to five different people on five different occasions. It multiplies the number of people you meet, which multiplies the sales you make, which multiplies your income and accelerates the speed at which you build your business.

Women host most shows, so in this book I refer to the person holding the show as the hostess.

Your hostess receives rewards, usually in the form of free products, substantial discounts, or exclusive gifts, depending on the sales and ongoing bookings generated from her show.

Most Party Plan companies offer hostess gifts for you to purchase at a low price, with which to reward your hostess. Other companies require you to report on the sales and bookings generated from each show, then they send the gift directly to the hostess along with her order. Alternatively, you can create your own reward program, purchasing product or gifts inexpensively, and selecting the most appealing rewards to motivate your hostesses.

Your hostess gets the pleasure of hosting her friends for an hour or two, with the entertainment laid on—you!

Coaching Your Hostess

First things first. Your hostess's role is to help you make the show a success, which is why she gets gifts and rewards. Your job is to help her succeed by coaching her properly.

Proper coaching will help prevent postponements and cancellations, ensure good attendance, and make the show more enjoyable and more effective.

Plan your day planner and To Do lists to include four coaching sessions for each hostess:

1. As soon as the show is booked
2. A week before the show
3. The day before the show
4. When you arrive to set up for the show

SESSION ONE

- As soon as the show is booked, enter the date and time in your day planner, together with the hostess's name, address, and phone number.
- Write down the date and time of the show for your hostess and discuss the theme or content of the show with her.
- Give her a hostess pack, including invitations to send to prospective guests. Your company will have relevant literature. If not, create your own.
- Show her the rewards she can receive. Help her choose one she especially likes and discuss the sales and bookings required to achieve it.
- Suggest she start building her guest list and brief her on what to say when inviting her guests.
- Encourage her to tell the guests that the show will be fun and informative (it's up to you to ensure that it is) and it will take no more than an hour and a half.
- Remind her to get a firm commitment from each guest. Suggest she use a phrase like, "I can only have five guests and I have reserved a place for you."

- Point out to your hostess the value of mixing her guests—different age groups and from different areas—as this increases the chances for more bookings than if all the guests are in the same circle of friends.
- Encourage her to overinvite. Cancellations and no-shows are inevitable.
- Ask her to keep refreshments simple. Elaborate snacks will discourage her guests from hosting their shows later.
- Send a confirmation letter, fax, or e-mail, thanking her in advance for the booking and reviewing the steps she must take for a successful show and the rewards she can expect to receive. A sample of this letter and a follow-up thank-you note are included at the end of this chapter.

Session Two

- Follow up a week before the show, to ensure your hostess has at least five guests confirmed. Remind her to invite two or three extras, to compensate for last minute cancellations. Share positive ideas with her to increase attendance, such as each guest bringing a friend.
- If she tries to cancel the show, ask: "How many guests do you have coming?" Then say, "It's too late for me to book another show for Wednesday. If there are fewer people, that means I can spend more time with the guests who are there. Relax, we're going to have a great time."
- Stress the importance of encouraging guests to arrive promptly, so the show can start and finish on schedule. A special gift, drawn for guests who have arrived on time, can work wonders.
- Give your hostess an incentive to collect outside orders (i.e., orders taken before the show) especially from guests who cancel at the last minute. She'll be motivated by the size and value of her hostess gift, which will depend on the total sales and bookings achieved. Remind her to look for future show bookings from those guests who can't make her particular show date, too.
- If it suits your style, work with her on the hostess "Tick Six" game. The game is fun and rewards your hostesses for putting preparation into the show booking. Offer it to each hostess as

added motivation, and you'll get the best possible show. Adapt it for your own business, with your own incentives, using the guideline at the end of this chapter as a prototype.

SESSION THREE

The night before the show, a nice touch is a quick call to your hostess to wish her well and cover any final points you think necessary. Remind her she still has time to invite a neighbor or a friend from work or family members, if the numbers are too low. Be enthusiastic and say how much you are looking forward to her show.

SESSION FOUR

- Immediately before the show, review the gift level she will be aiming for and how she can help achieve it, while you're setting up. Remind her not to serve snacks until your signal.
- If appropriate, plant a recruiting seed. Hostesses make great recruits.
- Find out about the guests attending so you can make your presentation relevant to them.
- Keep your enthusiasm at a high level. You have reserved this time especially for her. Never appear disappointed, no matter what the outcome of the evening. Think long-term. If your hostess thinks she has failed, she will never book another show. Believe she can do it, and let her know you believe in her.

Now, relax, enjoy yourself, and get on with the show!

Principles of Party Plan Business

There are principles to apply if you want to build a long-term successful Party Plan business. Follow the basic rules outlined below and your shows will all be hits.

KEEP IT SHORT

These days, people's lives are busier and their attention spans are shorter. Time is precious. Aim for no more than two hours from the moment you arrive until you're packing up to leave. This is a skill that takes resolve, discipline, and practice.

KEEP IT SIMPLE

We are constantly bombarded by messages from various sources, including television, radio, magazines, newspapers, billboards, mailings, the Internet, and unsolicited phone calls, and we have learned to shut down when we are not interested. By designing and following a simple format you will have your audience interested, intrigued, and wanting more. This leads to return invitations and ongoing bookings, where you can present fresh material to sustain interest.

KEEP IT COLORFUL

Black and white tells, color sells! Be animated, lively, and colorful. Involve your audience in your presentation. Use all the senses, including touch, smell, sight, sound, and even taste if appropriate. The more senses you excite, the more your audience will stay tuned in. Share stories and anecdotes to personalize your presentation. Use drama and humor. Don't forget, the more entertaining you are, the more warmly your message will be received. Even the most serious topics can be presented in a colorful way to keep your group entertained.

KEEP IT ACTIVE

Ask questions. Hand around products. Encourage the group to "try before they buy." This is ideal for cleaning products, clothing, cookware, cosmetics, giftware, jewelry, nutritional products, and most consumable lines. But don't turn your show into an elaborate training session, such as demonstrating complicated makeup techniques.

Keep It Duplicable

If you make it look easy, your guests will be able to picture themselves doing what you're doing. If your display is a designer masterpiece and your preparation takes too long, people may enjoy the show, but you'll have difficulty in getting repeat or referred bookings or sponsoring appointments. Your actions say, "This is all too hard." Don't arrive laden down with bags and boxes, as this is a major turn-off. Plus, you'll frighten your downline from doing shows if the effort appears to be too much.

Keep It Topical

People are most interested in what's new, different, and best. Keep up to date with the hottest topics and trends in your industry and incorporate these into your presentation. Nutritional supplements are a perfect example. These can be the dreariest products to sell or the liveliest, depending on your knowledge of current issues and your ability to share fresh, contemporary news that relates to your product line. Read relevant magazine and newspaper reports. Watch television documentaries, search the Internet, read all your company publications, and stay up-to-date with your industry. If you're selling cosmetics, keep up with the latest fashion looks through consumer magazines and adapt them to your customers.

Keep It Focused

A show is not a lecture, seminar, study course, or marathon. Be proud of your profession as a salesperson. You are at the show to find people to recruit into your downline, to book ongoing shows, and to make sales. Prepare yourself before every show by focusing on the exact outcome you want to achieve. I like to recommend a *One-Two-Three* approach. In order of importance, at each show aim for a minimum of:

One recruiting appointment;
Two future show bookings; and a minimum of
Three hundred dollars in sales.

When your mind is clearly focused, your thoughts will direct your words and actions toward getting the results you are focused on. Prepare yourself before you start every show by resolving to achieve *One-Two-Three*. Focus on it and you will achieve it! Not every time perhaps, but if you achieve it on average, you will be building a strong business.

Breaking Through Barriers to Bookings

Without future bookings, you have no business. Work on strategies to overcome the barriers that could be put up to prevent you filling your day planner with show bookings. Here are some examples of barriers and strategies:

"I don't have time to host a show." A show takes only two hours and appeals to busy people because it avoids the hassle and time taken to go shopping. A show can even be condensed into a lunch hour at the workplace, or held straight after work. Reinforce the hostess rewards that are available and compare their value with the small amount of time taken to make a few phone calls inviting guests.

"I don't know if my friends would be interested." You only need five people for a show. Keeping it small keeps it informal and fun. Small groups are best for individual attention. Ask each guest to invite a friend, and in turn have that friend bring another friend. Reward each guest who brings a friend with a gift. Your hostess then gets the opportunity to expand her circle of friends.

"My friends use other brands." Let your enthusiasm for your product and its uniqueness show through. Explain that you respect the opinions of people who use high-quality products and feel confident they will appreciate the quality of yours.

"My home is too small." That's just the way you like it. Intimate, relaxed, and fun. Remind her that she can also collect orders outside her show to count toward her hostess gift.

"My partner won't like the idea." Plan the show around the partner's schedule so it won't interfere. A quick show can be fitted into most schedules. Suggest a daytime show, or one run around the kitchen table, leaving the living room free.

"I work during the week and can't fit it in." Suggest a Saturday afternoon. This is especially ideal if you're selling cosmetics, as you can offer to give her a beauty makeover, ready for a glamorous night out.

"I'll have to ask my friends first." Explain the hassles she'll experience if she tries to juggle dates around different friends, trying to find one date that suits them all. Make a tentative date, giving her something specific to suggest to her friends. Remind her that for friends who can't make the nominated date she can take outside orders or even book a second show.

Dealing with Cancellations

A reality of network marketing is you have to cope with cancellations. Don't underestimate their impact on your business. Each show will open up new avenues for you, so the true impact of a lost booking is far more than the lost sales for that show. It's also the lost future bookings and recruiting opportunities that may have been generated from the show.

Cancellations interrupt your momentum, so adopt these techniques to help minimize them:

- Always book more shows than you want to do.
- Try not to book more than three to four weeks ahead.
- Stay in touch with your hostess between the booking and the show.
- Teach her to share your enthusiasm and tell her guests "I can't wait to see you on Tuesday night. I know we're going to have fun."

Some successful Party Planners have a waiting list in case of cancellations. Others have a list of potential hostesses who enjoy having shows at their homes. They receive a special extra gift for hosting an 11th-hour show. It's easier than you think. Your hostess has already been encouraged to make a list of whom she would invite, so she gets on the telephone, inviting her friends to a spontaneous show.

Alternatively, hold one yourself, inviting a few of your friends and best customers. As an incentive, guest's names could go into a drawing to win the hostess gift, as if it were their show.

If Party Plan is starting to sound a little complicated, don't despair. In the next chapter I will share with you the best blueprint I can offer. I use it to train people who want to get the best from Party Plan to sell and recruit. I call it Prime Time Party Plan.

Hostess "Tick Six" Game

Have your Hostess use this checklist for a successful Show. If she can tick off six of the eight steps to success, she will win a special gift (which you nominate, preferably product). Draw up your own sheet on your own letterhead with your company and/or product logo based on this guideline.

Tick off six items to win:

☐ 1. Hold show on date originally scheduled.
       Time.............. Date................

☐ 2. Five or more guests attending.

☐ 3. Sales of $300 or more.

☐ 4. Two confirmed bookings from your show.

☐ 5. Three guests I've never met.

☐ 6. Make an appointment to discuss joining
       my business.

☐ 7. Refer me to a friend who becomes
       interested in joining my business.

☐ 8. Have $100 in outside orders before your show.

Hostess Letters

Adapt these two sample letters to confirm and thank your hostess for helping you hold a great show.

Show Confirmation Letter:

Dear (*Hostess*),
Thank you for booking a (*type of*) show with me. I have reserved (*date*) from (*start time*) to (*finish time*) especially for you. It will be my pleasure to showcase our quality range of (*products*) to your friends and to present you with (*chosen hostess gift*) when we reach our target of (*required sales and future show bookings*).
To help make your show a success, I recommend you invite extra people to cover for last minute cancellations. Tell your guests that the show will take no longer than an hour and a half and will be informative and fun. Please call me at (*phone number*) if you have any questions. I look forward to seeing you on (*date*).

Warmest regards,

(*Your name*)

Show Follow-Up Letter:

Dear (*Hostess*),
Congratulations on the success of your show. I enjoyed meeting your friends and I am sure everyone will be happy with their product selections. I will deliver the products on (*date*) at (*time*). Please make any checks out to (*name details*).
I have pleasure in confirming (*details of hostess gift achieved*) to thank you for your contribution to a successful show. I hope we can do the same again soon.

Warmest regards,

(*Your name*)

CHAPTER 24

Prime-Time Party Plan

The people who come to your show have made a decision to forgo something else to be there. They could be relaxing at home with their family. They could be out having fun bowling, seeing a movie, or dining out. They could be enjoying a night's entertainment on television.

Your job is to ensure they're pleased they made the decision to come to your show.

We live in a world where everything's becoming more compressed. Movies, with the greatest storylines and starring the hottest celebrities, often last only 90 minutes. Popular television programs are as short as 30 minutes. A restaurant meal used to be a major night out. Now we pop into a cafe or restaurant for a quick bite or drive through without even getting out of our car.

When you tune into a television program, you decide before the first commercial break whether to stay with it or flick around for something more interesting. Keep this in mind when planning and presenting your show.

Although your guests won't walk out, they will mentally "leave the room" if you don't keep them entertained and interested. Include a few surprises in your show to reward their attendance and attention!

Prime-Time Party Plan works on the principles that apply to successful television programming. The purpose of a television program, whether it's news, entertainment, or documentary, is to deliver you, the viewer, to the advertisers, who wish to sell to you.

Similarly, with your show you provide news, entertainment, and information in return for the opportunity to advertise and sell your products and opportunity. You do this through commercials, which you intersperse through the program. It's a wonderful win-win-win arrangement, for your hostess, for you, and for the guests.

A Prime-Time Show

Let's go through a suggested format for a 7:00 P.M. show, step by step, as an example of how to keep it lively, interesting, and fun.

6:40, FINAL COACHING SESSION

Arrive 20 minutes early to set up your product display. Keep it simple. Conduct the final coaching session (Session Four) with your hostess to maximize results. Run through the format of the Show for her. Ask for a little information about each guest. You are partners, and the success of the evening will depend on both of you. Confirm the hostess reward she would like to aim for, to help generate enthusiasm about the show. Meet your guests as they arrive. Ask them questions about themselves. Learn their names.

7:00, THE OPENER

Start on time with a warm welcome, thanking your hostess and showing the guests the hostess rewards that can be earned tonight (your first commercial break!). Thank the guests for coming and assure them your presentation will take just an hour and a half. Ask all guests to tell you a little more about themselves, so they immediately feel involved. Outline the show's theme and the procedure for the evening. Present an exciting opener. (See the conclusion of this chapter for some opener suggestions.)

As with a television program or movie, it's vital to get your audience hooked to prevent them mentally from switching channels or switching off. In your first 10 minutes, work hard at making them want to know more. You can do this by asking thought-provoking questions, sharing news that relates to your product line, or by telling an interesting story. Humor is always appealing, so keep it lighthearted and lively. The point is get them tuned in to your topic.

7:15, COMMERCIAL BREAK

Now that you have them hooked, it's time for your next commercial break. Give a brief company profile. Keep it short and interesting. Share your own network marketing story. Briefly explain how you got started and what experiences and successes you have had.

You are your own best advertisement. Make sure you come across relaxed, happy, and successful.

Explain the benefits of starting your own network marketing business. Plant seeds by using phrases like, "If you want to know more, we'll make a time to meet for coffee," "I'm looking for people to train in the business, working full-time or part-time from home. You can earn $40 or more an hour." "If you like to travel, this is the best job ever." Let your enthusiasm show.

7:25, DEVELOP YOUR THEME

Develop the theme you have chosen to showcase your product. You may choose to demonstrate the product, involve your guests in a workshop where everyone tries the product, or pass the products around as you introduce them. Make sure you involve everyone and include a few surprises to hold their attention. Individualize your presentation, speaking to each guest by name, asking them questions, and offering specific advice and recommendations. Keep your presentation lively, with interesting facts, techniques, and anecdotes. You can develop these by listening to your sponsor, reading company material, and doing your own research.

Now is the time to create the desire to buy your products. Stay focused on achieving the *One-Two-Three* recruiting, booking, and sales goals you have set yourself.

7:50, RECRUITING AND BOOKINGS

Time for a couple more commercials, aimed at recruiting and bookings. Notice how, when you're watching television, you keep seeing the same commercials? This is because successful marketing companies know repetition works. Talk again enthusiastically about the benefits of having your own network marketing business, and mention the support and training given. For example, "What I love most about this business is how much support and encouragement I get," or "This is the best job I've ever had. I get paid to have a good time!" Offer guests the chance to host their own show and talk about the hostess rewards that are available.

7:55, THE FINALE

Complete your presentation, explain the ordering and delivery procedure, and ask for the sale. Be careful to leave them wanting more. Discuss different types of shows that can be booked. Often a question will arise that you can turn around to provide the perfect lead-in to a future show booking. Respond to the question by saying, "That's a great topic. We don't have time to cover it tonight, but let's have another show where we can explore it fully." Or, follow a skincare show by promoting the opportunity for a color workshop. Say, "Don't you just love all the new colors for summer? Next week/month I am offering all my clients color workshops on the new look. Who would like to book?" Don't be tempted to digress from the purpose of this show, especially at the expense of creating an opportunity to book another. Leaving your guests wanting more is your strongest opportunity to get bookings for new shows.

8:05, MEET THE STAR

Allowing three to five minutes per guest lets you finalize your product sales, pursue new show bookings, and follow up leads for recruitment interviews on a one-to-one basis, while your hostess is serving light refreshments. Hand out company literature, or your own presentation binder (see Chapter 25), for guests to read while they are waiting to talk with you. Don't fall into the trap of letting one or two people dominate your time. Be sure to spend time talking with every one of your guests before you lose them. At the conclusion of this segment, add up the sales and bookings generated.

8:30, THANK YOU

Thank your hostess and the guests, and talk about the gift your hostess has achieved. Also thank the guests who have booked their own show or made an appointment to discuss the business opportunity. Start to pack up your display.

8:40, AND GOODNIGHT

The show's over and you're leaving. In two hours you have presented a lively, upbeat show, made product sales, made new show bookings, and booked at least one recruitment interview. You have
successfully adopted my motto for a successful show, "Be Brief, Be
Effective, Be Gone!"

The Review

After every show comes the review. Just like a show opening on
Broadway, the latest movie, or the new season's television program, we
live or die by our reviews.

In Party Plan, the results are your best reviews. But you can also be
your own reviewer by analyzing how you could make each show better
than the last. The more you do, the better you'll become.

Imagine how strong your business will be if every show produces a
minimum of two future bookings, and if everyone in your downline produces two bookings from every show they do!

The best booking tool is a great show, so after each show, ask yourself these seven questions:

1. "What did I do to motivate people to book another show?" Did
   you leave them, like a good television drama, "hanging on the
   cliff edge," wanting to find out more?
2. "Was my show fun and informative?" Did you include lots of
   hands-on involvement during the show, or did you act as if your
   guests were in a classroom and you were the teacher? When
   you let people try the product, they buy the product. Would you
   buy clothing from the store window without trying it on first in
   front of the mirror!
3. "How did I come across?" Were you a shining advertisement for
   your product, your company, and for the magic of network marketing? Did you look, sound, and act as a friendly, relaxed, and
   confident businessperson?
4. "Did I give them something new?" Your guests gave up something to spend time with you. Did they leave your show feeling

entertained, better informed, and rewarded for giving up their time to attend?

5. "How were my pace and timing?" Did you keep the show moving along and lively? People remember your opening and your close more than anything else. Did you start and finish on time?

6. "Did I close the sale?" Did you ask for the sale? Your show was to generate product orders, new show bookings, and recruiting interviews. Don't be so eager to please and entertain that you overlook the *One-Two-Three* goals you set yourself for the show. Always ask for the sale.

7. "Was my hostess coaching effective?" Did you go through all the coaching steps? If you take a shortcut, you'll get a less than optimum result.

When you give yourself an overall review of the show, take some credit, too. You're the writer, director, and performer! The best way to keep improving your performance is to build on your strengths while gently chipping away at and improving the weaker points of your presentation until you're totally relaxed, polished, and professional.

Keeping It Personal

I try to introduce an opportunity for my audience to participate in a self-discovery exercise in everything I do. The beauty industry lends itself very well to this, as your audience is involved in discovering, for example:

- What's my skin type?
- What's my beauty "personality"?
- What's my color "season"?
- What's my skin's potential for premature aging?
- What are my best colors?
- What's my face (or eye) shape?
- What are my best features?
- What's my fragrance personality?

The choices are limitless. If you're selling fashion, health, or nutritional products there are even more games you can play to keep your customers and recruits involved in a voyage of self-discovery that will lead to confident product choices, happy customers, and a competent downline.

Great Show Openers

The following suggestions may help get your mind working on winning ways to open your show. I have based these on openers I know work for the cosmetic industry. Use them as thought starters and adapt them to your product range.

You could open a makeup show with:

Did you know that each of us has a perfect look? It's true. We each have our own beauty personality and the secret is to choose the colors, textures, and techniques that best compliment what nature gave us. Tonight, I'm going to show you how to discover your beauty personality and how to make the most of your natural beauty style.

You could open a skincare show for a mature group with:

Did you know that up to 80 percent of skin aging is premature, preventable, and, in some cases, even reversible? Today, no one needs to accept dull, sagging skin and wrinkles as inevitable. Because we now know what causes skin aging, we can protect against it. Tonight, I'm going to show you how to keep your skin beautiful, youthful, and glowing.

Even a younger audience can be intrigued by the same topic, if you position it accurately:

How many of you expect to look exactly like your mother when you're her age? (Allow time for response, probably a few laughs.) *While we all tend to inherit our parents' features, I like to call you the lucky generation, because we now know so much more about the skin and why it ages than we did in your mother's day. Chances are, if you take care of your skin as I show you tonight, you will look up to 10 years younger than your mother when you're her age. How does that sound?*

I have presented these workshops to both large and small groups and they are guaranteed audience pleasers. All women want to look "a little younger, a little more beautiful" so these topics never fail to amuse and intrigue. Above all, because they are learning about themselves, everyone leaves feeling more confident about the products I have helped them select.

Similar introductions could be used for nutritional supplements, focusing on the effects of stress, poor diet, pollution, smoking, and other lifestyle excesses. Few people can resist the opportunity to learn more about themselves and how they can improve their lives.

Use these introductions as idea starters to develop the appropriate show openers for your products.

CHAPTER 25

Recruiting from Shows

Shows are a fertile ground into which you plant your recruiting seeds. If yours is a one-to-one business, it isn't very different.

To be serious about recruiting, every time you make a product presentation, include a commercial on joining the business.

In network marketing everything happens because you make it happen. Always be on the lookout for the people who will drive your business in the future. If you do a show without asking at least one person to join the business, or to meet with you and discuss the opportunity, your business will fail. People come and go in network marketing, and you have to keep fueling the fire of your business with new recruits. Because you never know when you are going to meet a person who wants to join your business, remember the little phrase:

"Anyone, anytime, anyplace, always *ask*!"

Your Hostess

With shows, your prospects are both your hostess and the guests. Naturally, your hostess is your hottest prospect. Here's why:

- She is interested enough in the product to host the show for you.
- She has friends and enjoys socializing.
- She is a natural leader to whom people respond (they turned up to her show, didn't they?).
- You have many opportunities to build one-on-one rapport with her before, during, and after the show.

If you think your hostess has an interest in joining your downline, share with her details of what you will earn if her show's sales target is reached. Hearing an actual dollar figure can act as a powerful catalyst to heighten her interest in your business opportunity.

The Guests

Before the show, when you ask your hostess about the guests who are coming, ask about those who may be interested in the opportunity to earn extra income. This will get her thinking about the guests and about which of them she could sign up if and when she gets started.

When the guests arrive, make sure you meet each one individually. Introduce yourself by name and make a conscious effort to remember their names. I always find it helps to repeat the name a few times as I talk to a new person.

There's nothing wrong with using inexpensive stick-on nametags either. You can always make light of your forgetfulness or make a game of it by giving guests a fun adjective before their name, for example, Marvelous Marilyn and Awesome Angela. If your guests are extroverted, they could make up the descriptive adjective themselves, with a prize for the most creative. (The prize doesn't have to be expensive—chocolate never fails to appeal.) This is a lighthearted icebreaker, helps everyone get to know each other (especially you), and works toward your objective of making the event fun as well as informative.

The time you spend getting to know the guests before the start of each show will help you target your presentation more effectively and determine levels of interest. Before opening the show try to identify one or two guests—especially those recommended by your hostess— who could be good prospects. These are often the bright, lively, confident people who stand out from the rest. As the show progresses, keep an eye out for those who are helping their friends make selections or giving them encouragement and positive reinforcement. These are the people you want in your business, but don't dismiss any prospect on first meeting. It's true that still waters can run deep. Work hard to develop your skills in spotting potential. It will help you become an effective recruiter.

Don't be afraid to be direct. Most people will be flattered that you think they would be great in the business. You never know how many are thinking, "I wish someone had asked me," but it takes your initiative to start the ball rolling.

Planting Seeds

As your show progresses, plant more seeds throughout your product demonstration during the commercial breaks. They can be casual comments like, "This is what I love about my business. Meeting new friends, having fun and getting paid for it" or "The company is taking us all overseas in May for a fabulous seminar." This comment could be made stronger by adding "If any of you love traveling, make sure you talk to me later." When it's appropriate, don't hesitate to talk about something particularly pertinent to your achievements. For example, "This is a special month for me, as I have just earned my first company car." Use any achievements or rewards that have made the month special for you.

If you have established empathy with people, you'll know some may feel a little unsure about their ability. Overcome this in advance with comments like, "A year ago I wouldn't have believed I would be doing this and enjoying it so much."

A successful, inexpensive, and professional way to reinforce your seed messages is to have them framed as small displays. Print out the pertinent messages and mount them into picture frames. Inexpensive frames are widely available in a range of sizes, styles, and colors to coordinate with your product display.

Here are some idea starter seeds that work:

- Earn extra money in your spare time. Ask me how.
- Start your own business
- Apply now to join our next trip to
  (. . . *your international seminar destination*)
- Earn extra money for Christmas. Ask me how.
- Enthusiastic people wanted to train as (*Beauty, Nutrition, etc.*) Consultants. No experience necessary.
- Part-time work available.
- Become a Nutritional Consultant. Ask me how.
- Ask me about becoming a Beauty Consultant.

Another great idea is to purchase a photo album or binder and create a presentation book highlighting your experiences and achievements as an independent distributor. Include seminars, functions, rewards earned, new car presentations, international travel, and similar events. Guests can pass the book around and browse at their leisure. Tuck response slips into the back page for guests to complete and indicate their interest in finding out more about joining you in your business.

Don't be coy about the fact you are making money. Most of the people who join you will do so for one reason—they want to bring more money into their household. That's why comments like "Doing this has made me financially independent" and "I can show you how to become financially independent, too" are productive seeds to plant.

Just keep planting those seeds in the room. "If you think you might like to do this, talk to me later" and "These are great products, but I'm happy to share with any of you our best offer—the business (or income) opportunity."

Be Patient

Don't expect seeds to burst forth into flower as soon as you plant them. Their purpose is to give your hostess and guests the idea that they could do what you're doing. Make the most of every opportunity to talk about how the business has changed your lifestyle. Tell true stories about the fun you had starting out, the learning you went through, and the successes you have achieved. If you are new to the business, talk about the changes you've seen in other people's lives.

As you plant your seeds, you'll find the words *when you* are effective in helping the seeds grow. For example, "When you start" and "When you join."

It's a good idea to include a "check the box" section on the customer order or response slip, offering more information about the business opportunity. At the end of your show, invite them to check the box and reiterate, "If you would like to talk more about the business opportunity, please tell me. There's no obligation, but I would love to meet over coffee and share the details with you."

Don't be afraid to be bold and forthright. "You would be great doing this" or "I'd love to work with you" and "Let's meet and discuss this more" are all approaches that work. Your enthusiasm will be contagious and your confidence will strengthen theirs. As the seeds take root, keep nurturing them.

Some people cloak their lack of confidence in words such as, "I don't think I could do it" or "I don't have the time." Often this means they're looking to you to tell them they will be good enough. They're seeking your reassurance and want you to show them how easily they can get started and fit the opportunity into their schedule.

It's up to you to remove the barriers that prevent them from taking the first step. Every barrier you remove clears the path for a new distributor to join your business.

You are always your own best advertisement for the business opportunity. If it looks too hard or complicated, you'll scare people away. Keep it simple, keep it fun, keep them thinking, "I could do this."

After the Show

When your presentation is over, talk directly with your hostess and your guests. While you're thanking your hostess for her hospitality and finalizing her hostess gift, share with her again how much money she could have made if she had done the show. Show her the sales you achieved and the commission earned. If you have new shows booked from her show, encourage her to join before those bookings and promise to run the first shows with her. She can help more and more with each show. Doing them together will be a stronger and faster way for her to learn than you just telling her about it.

Reinforce your confidence in her ability to be successful. And reassure her that you and the company will give her full support, including training, to help her gain competence and confidence.

Don't be concerned about losing your commission off those shows. Your commission on her subsequent activity will repay your investment handsomely. Always take the long-term view.

Use her shows to teach her how to recruit, too. The sooner she sees results, the stronger and more confident she will feel. If you can have her recruiting and building her own downline within the first four weeks, she'll be convinced of the potential. These first four weeks are critical. Plan to invest as much of your time as possible in supporting and developing your new recruit from the early stages.

During your earlier conversation you will have learned something about your hostess that indicates how useful the extra income will be—a family holiday, overseas trip, renovations to the house, repairs to a car, children's education, or maybe a new wardrobe. You can easily reinforce how joining you will enable her to earn the extra money. But remember, it's not the money itself, it's the benefit of the money that matters.

It's the same with guests you have identified as prospects. If there's good energy in the air, you may get a commitment at the show. But don't be too anxious about getting everything done immediately. It is usually more appropriate to make appointments to get to know each new prospect better, to develop empathy and understanding, and to overcome any apprehensions they may have.

Whatever approach you choose to use, always have the date set for the first training session. "In your training, I will cover everything you will need to know for getting started. The first session will be held (*specific date and time*)." Your organization and preparedness will demonstrate professionalism and engender the confidence needed to bring people along with you.

Planning Checklist—
the Secret of Great Shows

Use these key points as a checklist to help make every show a great show.

- Never turn up and think, "It'll be all right on the night." I cannot overemphasize the need to plan each show thoroughly.
- Plan your opening. Always have a strong start, giving an overview of the benefits of network marketing. Remind your guests that you offer hassle-free shopping and a chance to try before they buy in a social environment where they are pampered, not pressured.
- Include reference to the benefits of a convenient, time-saving alternative to shopping through retail outlets, the television, or the Internet.
- Plant seeds in your guests' minds throughout the show about why they should each book their own show and what rewards they can receive as the hostess.
- Plan to find someone to recruit. And, most importantly . . .
- End your show with a quick but strong recap. There is one sure way to let your guests feel they will have a great time if they book a show with you. It's to give them a great time at this one.

PART SEVEN

Million-Dollar

Leadership

CHAPTER 26

Aim to Be Outstanding

Chances are you were or will be sponsored or recruited into network marketing by another distributor. If you are fortunate, that person will have the skills, experience, and desire to help you grow.

However, responsibility for your success ultimately remains with you. You can't afford to let your success depend on how good your upline sponsor is. The sturdiest plants often grow in the harshest conditions, and the most beautiful flowers bloom in the desert. So, if you feel you don't have a great upline, the best answer is to learn from your experience and become a great upline for your own people.

Your Job as a Leader

You are not going to make a million without a large, productive team. As the leader of your team, one of your roles will be to constantly work on changing your people's belief systems, taking each of them through the stages of hoping they can make a success of it, to knowing they can, and then realizing their dreams.

That means working on raising both self-esteem and skill levels.

As a member of your downline becomes more competent, they will become more confident, which in turn brings more competence. It's a wonderful carousel to ride on.

One of your key roles as a leader is to set the example others follow. Work hard at developing your own talent and character as part of training yourself. Surround yourself with people who think like you, are aiming at what you're aiming at, and have the same purpose in life. In the T-shirt and bumper sticker language of today, "You can't soar like an eagle when you're surrounded by turkeys."

Develop your own passion for excellence. Take an interest in the good things in life. Read stimulating books. See the best movies. Surround yourself with upbeat, high-energy, positive people. It makes sense to have role models; it's part of human nature. When you choose your environment, choose the positive.

Before long, you'll notice that you are leading your downline the same way. You'll be developing a team of leaders who attract strong and successful people to join your group. Your success can come only when you have this strength behind you. Pushing them toward success will propel you there, too.

Don't be nervous of leadership. People seek leadership, and your recruits will be looking to you to guide and teach them. As you start to train, you'll find the skills you are imparting to others are being strengthened in yourself.

The more you teach, the more you learn.

Empower Your Recruits

Don't fall into the trap of doing for others instead of teaching and encouraging them to do for themselves. The secret is to empower people in your downline to succeed on their own.

If you are doing the work for them, you are wasting time that can be better used for personal prospecting and selling. Plus, you are sending the wrong signals to your downline.

They want to be like you. You want to duplicate yourself in them. So you must teach them the three key steps of business building:

1. Selling product
2. Prospecting and recruiting
3. Training and developing

All the time, you are gently leading them to independence. Know when to step back. Don't lose sight of the fact that unless you keep selling and recruiting you won't keep your own business vibrant. The same applies to your downline. You can't recruit when you're being a nursemaid.

Think what happens every year in nature when the mother bird pushes her young from the nest. The time comes for all of us when we must fend for ourselves, find our own wings and fly. Your role is to know when to start weaning and moving toward the time when you let them fly. Train your downline to do the same with their recruits.

It has been said that the secret of good leadership is to listen, learn, help, and lead. I believe the secret of *outstanding* leadership is even harder. It's to listen, learn, help, and *leave*. It's only when you learn the right time to step back that you can truly empower people. Achieve this and everyone in your downline will be able to achieve their full potential.

A Strong Partnership

Not every new recruit will be as successful as you wish, because not everyone has the same definition of, or desire for, success. Nor will they all have the necessary motivation or energy to succeed big time.

When you recruit a new person into network marketing you are offering them a partnership, an opportunity to share the rewards of success while making a contribution to your business. This takes commitment from both sides. Your commitment is to share your knowledge, skills, experience, and time. Their commitment is to produce results by applying the skills you give them.

A one-sided partnership quickly leads to disappointment, frustration, and failure.

Ask these questions of your recruits before you commit to mentoring a new person, to ensure that you give your support to those who are willing to work and make a commitment.

1. What are the most important things you want to achieve from this business?
2. What income level will you require to achieve these?
3. How much time are you prepared to commit to your business each week?
4. Are you willing to give your business three to five years to succeed?

Get these answers in writing if possible, but always discuss it with them. Once you have established the level of commitment your new person is prepared to make, you can match your commitment to theirs and go on with the relevant training and support program.

Let your new recruits know that you are committed to helping them become as successful as they, not you, want to be. Don't waste time working with people who are unwilling to work or not prepared to do what it takes to be successful. Avoid nursing one leg of your business at the expense of the rest. I have seen many leaders slip into this trap, hoping they can bring a weak part of their business back to good health by spending extra time on it.

It is far more effective to build on your strengths.

What can happen in network marketing is the people in your down-line who demand the most, and take up most of your time, produce the least for you.

Instead of supporting the weak, you will find it's far more profitable to focus your energies on working with people who have a sincere desire to succeed, are serious about the business, and are making the effort. They will quickly identify themselves to you by their actions.

"Checkerboard" Development

There is an effective game you can play during the development stage of your new recruits. It's one I call "Checkerboard" or "Your Move, My Move."

Think of their development as a strategic, step-by-step process. You make the first move by giving them their first training, together with agreed next steps. Now it's their move, to implement the lessons of your training. When this happens, take them through the next training step, and so on.

At the initial stage there's no need to give them a wealth of infor-mation beyond the key benefits of your product line, how to build their prospect list, and how to make calls and get bookings. Once your pro-tégé has achieved the tasks you set, they are ready to proceed to the next training step.

START WITH A LAUNCH

An effective way to start training is to do the first bookings with your new recruit, starting with a business launch. Use it to officially cel-ebrate the opening of your new recruit's business and present the opportunity to invited guests. An official business launch will help to generate excitement, give the new business credibility, allow you to target the best prospects for recruiting and booking, set a standard for the future of the new business, and give valuable support to your new recruit. The alternative—letting your new recruit stumble through the most critical part of their business alone—will most likely see the new business failing to get off the ground.

Your professional presentation to your new recruit's best friends and associates will ensure a healthy start.

Try also to do the first show, the first one-on-one presentation, and the first recruiting interview with all new recruits. This guarantees their hottest prospects have the benefit of your expertise, while allowing your recruit to learn on the job.

At the same time, ensure your new recruit attends all training available to them. Encourage them to do their homework after each training session, revising the notes and putting into practice the skills taught. Start each new training session with a brief review of the previous one. Don't give out too many notes (always give them out after your presentation, not during it, so attendees are not distracted from what you are saying). Keep your training handouts clear, concise, and uncluttered. Don't copy them to death. Keep fresh master copies to ensure your presentations are always professional looking.

THE FIRST MONTH

The first month for a new network marketer is the most critical. During this first month, support and encourage them, with both of you working together to get the momentum going. Maximize the opportunities produced by their hot list of prospects while the list is still hot. Unless you build momentum quickly, your new recruits will falter. The second start-up will be much harder, as they will have depleted their list of initial contacts.

You will have more chance of achieving success if your new recruits have clear expectations and specific deadlines, backed by training, structured support, and feedback.

If the first month is successful, they will continue to maintain the level of interest and excitement needed to drive the business forward. Momentum is everything, and there's nothing like the buildup of energy in the first month to start it rolling.

You can expect to lose some new recruits who fail to fire in the first month, so develop a specific support program for all new recruits.

In the first few weeks follow up and review every appointment held by your new recruit.

- What was the goal?
- What was the result?
- What was done well?
- What was weak or omitted?

If no further bookings were achieved, did the new recruit remember to include the job talk advertisement in the presentation? Did she ask for bookings? You will be surprised how many forget to ask, as they suffer from opening night nerves.

Mostly, when a less than successful result has been achieved, it's because the recruit varied the format, or forgot a key part of the presentation. By conducting a post mortem after every appointment, you can identify and remedy mistakes before they start to affect the ongoing success of the new business.

Step by Step

Make sure you train your downline at the appropriate levels and remind them you are not a teacher or a trainer. You are there to help them develop their business. Offering the incentive to move up to a more advanced group will be a great motivator for the right people.

Your new recruit deserves every opportunity you can provide to achieve their highest potential. The step up you give them at the beginning is a vital part of their development.

Leadership Effectiveness Self-Test

Are you the best you can be? Are you providing a strong role model to your customers and downline? Use this self-test to see how you can be better.

How I am probably seen by
my customers:

_____

_____

_____

_____

_____

_____

I am probably seen by
my downline:

_____

_____

_____

_____

_____

_____

How I would like to be seen by
my customers:

_____

_____

_____

_____

_____

_____

How I would like to be seen by
my downline:

_____

_____

_____

_____

_____

_____

Steps I will take to bridge the gap:

_____

_____

_____

_____

_____

Steps I will take to bridge the gap:

_____

_____

_____

_____

_____

As your leadership skills develop, use these evaluating exercises in your downline training sessions, to help your team improve their performance, too.

CHAPTER 27

The Training Game

The measure of your ability as a leader is your willingness to share your skills. Because network marketing is a formula that works, you don't have to reinvent the wheel. While it's not a franchise business, like McDonald's for example, the tools that work are simple, standard, and duplicable.

Work the formula and you will soon be on your way to selling a million, then earning a million.

Your Training Program

It goes without saying that education is one of the keys to success in any business.

Your ability to motivate will be considerably strengthened by your ability to give your recruits the tools they need to achieve success through training.

How you help your people develop will make a large contribution toward their success, but ultimately people are responsible for their own action or lack of action.

Let's look closely at the elements of a successful training program.

SHARING IN THE VISION

The brightest flame is hardest to extinguish. Involve everyone early on in creating the vision—a pride in the business, the company, the products, and the reason why they're in network marketing. Uncover their individual dream and strive to keep it alive. The more vividly you paint the picture, the stronger will be their desire to participate in it and the longer it will last through the ups and downs that lie ahead.

SETTING CLEAR EXPECTATIONS

Always set clear expectations. When clear expectations are in place, most people will try to meet them. Have your downline stretching for attainable targets, ones built upon a combination of their own abilities and desires and the time they have available to work their business.

SKILLS TRAINING

Provide the skills and knowledge your downline needs to master the maze that network marketing can be. Focus on training to successfully perform the key skills that create successful network marketers— planning, booking, selling, prospecting, recruiting, training, leading, and developing.

ONGOING SUPPORT AND COMMUNICATION

Establish a routine of ongoing communication and support, until you know they are ready to stand alone. This is especially critical in the first three months as they master the skills.

RECOGNITION OF RESULTS

Be generous with recognition to reinforce the activities that are producing success. People thrive on recognition, so make every step in their development a milestone.

Training the New Recruit

In each of the first four months take your new recruit through the process of learning and acquiring the skills they need to be in control of their own business and their own success.

Your program will look like this:

Month One: The *structured training stage*, including plenty of opportunities to observe you in action.
Month Two: The *learning stage*, where they start finding their feet with your close contact, encouragement, and feedback.

Month Three: The *doing stage*. By this time they are able to work on their own, mastering the skills and developing the confidence that will make them successful. They still need your support, but less so.

Month Four: The *consolidating and developing stage*. Now they are starting to see the results and enjoy the rewards.

Your training will put the new recruit's prospects in the right perspective. On the one hand they need to know that it takes hard, consistent work to develop a customer base and recruit their own downline. But on the other hand, you should also engender excitement about network marketing's unlimited potential.

Try to read your new recruits carefully, by questioning and listening, listening, listening. Some will have joined for fun or a love of the product. Others may appear a little offhand, "It didn't cost me much to join, so I don't have much to lose." Still others will be extremely keen to make a fantastic success of it.

You might also recognize some people with real potential who underestimate their own ability to succeed. These are the ones whose growth, development, and success will surprise, given the right training, encouragement, support, and leadership.

Don't lose sight of the fact that your ultimate goal is to develop your new recruits to the stage when they are duplicating you in recruiting and training their own downline who, in turn, will recruit and train their own downline.

Nuts and Bolts

During initial training there are the nuts and bolts to cover. They are listed below. However, remember that much of what we do is based on emotion, rather than purely on the practical. Therefore, the emotional side of training must be covered, too.

Include:

- Your expectations of them and the expectations they have of themselves. In most cases they will initially set goals far lower than they can achieve, because they don't yet know their full potential or the full potential of network marketing. Conversely, your new recruit will sometimes have unrealistic expectations in relation to the time that they are prepared to invest. Bringing them back to earth, to ensure they are not set up for disappointment, is equally valuable.

- Goal setting for 7 days, 30 days, 60 days, and 90 days. Then for one, three, and five years. Set deadlines together. And let them know you'll be constantly following up, to help them meet their commitments and to give them recognition when they do.
- Time management, instilling a sense of discipline and seriousness about success.
- Knowledge of the company. If your company's products have a "story," this is the time to bring it to life in a way your people can duplicate when they, in turn, recruit and train.
- Thorough training on the products or services, including who they are targeted toward and the benefits of using them.
- How to build a prospect list for customers and recruits.
- How to get the first and ongoing bookings.
- The importance of referrals and how to ask for them.
- How prospecting and recruiting work, by both role-playing and having them sit in on some of your recruitment and sales presentations. The quicker you help them recruit their own people, the sooner they will be able to do it without you.
- Basic sales techniques, including Party Plan if you are using it.
- The value of consistent servicing and how to manage it.
- Revision of company literature and materials they will use in their business.
- How to fill out the forms. Every company has procedures for ordering and for registering new recruits.
- How to develop and operate their customer and downline files.
- The importance of attending all training sessions and company-sponsored functions, including opportunity meetings, and of bringing prospective recruits.
- Personal skills, including professional image and communications.
- A briefing on the technologies you and your company use.

Getting it right from the start will make everyone's life happier. I recommend you complete their first order with them, preferably at your first training. You'll ensure they're doing it right while having another opportunity to review the products and reinforce the success of their first order.

Advanced Training

From the fourth month onward, your new recruits will be ready to actively participate in regular team meetings. Don't fall into the trap of overtraining. Once a month is enough.

A key advantage of group training is the efficiency. It's more effective to train once with six or eight people in one meeting than to repeat it six or eight times with a different person each time.

Formal, structured training and on-the-job training are part of the duplication process that makes network marketing successful.

Be careful, though, that you don't confuse your newer people by involving them in advanced training too soon.

Plan training sessions on a regular basis and ensure all your people mark them in their diaries.

Making It Fun

Here are two fun ideas for product sales and recruitment, to help make your training come alive. Try them with your downline from time to time, to keep your business driving forward.

Product Drive
This quick and easy competition is perfect to run with your team during a slow selling period. Everyone selects his or her favorite product from the range, or you select one for the group. At training, encourage each to present a two- to three-minute sell of the product as a dress rehearsal.

Then, during the following week, the person who sells the most of their personal favorite, or your nominated product of the week, wins a prize. A competition is always a great motivator, and your team will be earning while they're learning, while they're having fun.

I find this technique successful when I want to boost sales in a particular week or for a particular promotion. It's easy for your team to respond to, it's fun, and it works wonders!

Recruitment Drive
Another idea is to run a competition among your team when sponsoring slows down. After a training session on sponsoring, declare an "Everyone Gets One" week. The goal is for everyone in your downline to introduce one new person to the business during the following seven days. Everyone. This really sharpens their focus and puts the training ideas and skills into immediate action. An ideal prize is to take those who achieve it to a special dinner. Run this promotion successfully and your team could double overnight!

If you feel that your people need extra support and encouragement to make it through the promotion, pair each person with another, so they can compete as a team, still aiming for "Everyone Gets One."

CHAPTER 28

Walking in Their Shoes

As your downline develops, you'll learn something about the people in it: you cannot dictate their behavior.

You can motivate people with your excitement. You can influence them with your enthusiasm. You can train them in product information and selling skills. But they are free-spirited people, just like you, who joined a network marketing business for the freedom it offers, just as you did.

Lead Through Understanding

Develop the art of listening to and connecting with the feelings and motivations of the people around you. It will help you develop the empathy that builds trust, and relationships built on that trust.

You will be a great leader when you see, understand, genuinely care about, and believe in the potential that lies within each person in your downline.

Empowering others starts by understanding them. We are not all created the same. We don't all react to the same situation the same way. We don't all have an equal amount of potential for growth. But we all have potential to grow more.

You can push people, but real leaders are out front, providing the inspiration to move forward by clearing the path, anticipating and removing the obstacles that may stop their people from achieving true potential.

Much has been written on personality types. Developing your skills in accurately recognizing and responding to different personalities will help you become a better salesperson and a better leader.

When you begin to understand other people, you can identify which hot buttons to push in order to lead them. You do it by "walking in their shoes."

Personality Types

Personalities vary across a wide spectrum, from those who make decisions 100 percent emotionally to those who rationally plot every move, with limitless shades of difference in between. There are as many different personality types as there are people, so be careful you don't put people in boxes.

The following guidelines may help you identify and respond to some of the more common personality types and enhance your ability to communicate effectively:

DOUBTERS

Doubters listen to everything you say, then predictably reply with the word *But* . . . "But what if I hold a show and no one shows up?" "But what if no one likes the product?" Doubters may frustrate you with their caution, uncertainty, and craving for reassurance. You can help them by accentuating the positive, eliminating the negative, and supporting with plenty of reassurance. For example, "The product is fully guaranteed, so if your customer is not happy, the company will refund your money."

EMOTIONALS

Emotionals need the comfort of knowing they are valued. How you say things often means more than what you say. Keep Emotionals involved and feeling important. They can easily misinterpret nuances, so tread softly, you tread on their dreams. You know you have them on your side when they say, "It just feels right!"

ENTHUSIASTS

Don't you love Enthusiasts! Eager to embrace anything new, different, and exciting, they're open to fresh ideas and are quick to spot an opportunity. Enthusiasts are easy to sell to and easy to involve in your network marketing business, provided you keep their interest. Easily sidetracked by anything new and exciting on the horizon, they may lack the ability to stay on course. Keep feeding them with new ideas and new challenges and you'll have a charismatic leader in your team whose enthusiasm is infectious.

FREEDOMS

A Freedom floats through life as a free, unfettered spirit. Often infuriatingly unconventional to others, they are creative and love to rewrite the rules and live life on their own terms. Freedoms respond well to the less structured environment of network marketing.

INDEPENDENTS

Independents are self-contained and self-reliant and prefer to do things their own way, in their own time. They need a sense of self-sufficiency and prefer to feel they are making their own decisions. Give them information, give them space then watch them grow.

NESTERS

Nesters lack security, depending on others for support, often asking, "What do you think?" to make up for their lack of self-confidence. Your challenge is to draw them out and gently lead them toward independence. They will be the last to leave the nest, but can fly high when properly nurtured. You need a quiet, subtle approach with Nesters or you may scare them away. Loyalty to you, your company, and others in the team will be one of their greatest strengths.

PLEASERS

Eager to gain approval, Pleasers are quick to volunteer to contribute whenever they can and are happiest when they feel appreciated for their efforts. While Pleasers are easygoing and amiable, be wary that they often feel the need to mother, not manage, their downline.

POWERHOUSES

Powerhouses want everyone to be reasonable and do it their way. Controlling personalities who like to be in command, they'll seek time in the limelight. Be careful not to let them overwhelm or crowd out others. Difficult to manage, yes, but once you have won over a Powerhouse they make dynamic leaders.

QUIET ACHIEVERS

Quiet Achievers can be deceptive, as they don't push themselves forward. They're good listeners and quietly take in all that's going on around them. They can easily be overlooked when in the company of more outgoing personalities, but their calm inner strength can produce a determined, hardworking network marketer.

RATIONALS

Rationals are hungry for data, statistics, and facts. You won't win them over with hype or puffery. With Rationals, "tell, don't sell." It pays to be diligent in doing your homework for this personality type. Supply the figures, deadlines, and guidelines they need to make a considered decision. Rationals will recognize and respond well to the business potential of network marketing.

SEEKERS

Seekers aspire to status and success. Whether it's a product choice or their status within your company, they seek recognition of their achievements and love the incentives, cars, and travel benefits of network marketing.

SOCIAL-LIGHTS

Social-Lights are bright lights who attract others. They love being around other people, and people love being around them. Charismatic, generous, and warm, they make great network marketers, as they effortlessly attract customers and build their own downline. Social-

Lights also make great hostesses and Party Plan sellers. Always keep an eye out for them.

Successful leadership is about recognizing and responding to diverse and different personality types. There's risk in taking a one-size-fits-all approach to others. Work hard to become not just a good listener but a communicator who has, and shows, genuine empathy with other people. There's power in putting yourself into other people's shoes.

Training the Trainers

As your success in network marketing comes from duplicating yourself, make sure you take time to train the trainers. The more you train your downline to duplicate your actions, the quicker they will train and develop their own downline.

People learn by doing, so get your people involved in and contributing to training. Resist the temptation to stand at the front of the room and lecture. Use role-playing and practical workshops to teach skills. Brainstorming is ideal to plan a strategy or event because, first, you don't have all the ideas or answers and, second, when people come up with ideas, they feel ownership of them. There's serendipity in a group, too, where the whole is more than the sum of all the parts. As you spark off each other, magical ideas appear.

We learn and remember what we do far more than what we read or hear. Rather than talking to your people or drowning them in handouts, bring things to life through involvement. Have your people up on their feet talking about their experiences, to help them become used to speaking in public in front of a friendly audience.

Product knowledge presented as a fun quiz or in a game show format will be more interesting than straight learning. I often borrow the theme of popular television game shows to present training sessions that are lively and entertaining. There are endless ways to make your training lively and fun, as well as informative. All it takes is a little imagination and a little preparation beforehand.

Personality Workshop

Try this three-step training exercise to get your downline team involved in identifying and responding to different personality types.

Start by giving an outline, using the guidelines in this chapter or in your own words, on the importance of recognizing that we all have different personalities and respond to different approaches.

Step 1. *Guess Who?*

Give each participant an envelope with the name of a personality type inside; Doubter, Emotional, Enthusiastic, Freedom, Independent, Nester, Pleaser, Powerhouse, Quiet Achiever, Rational, Seeker, and Social-Light.

The brief is for each participant to role-play a one-minute characterization of the personality type they are representing. The others try to correctly identify the personality type portrayed and then discuss how best to work with that type of person.

Step 2. *Who's Who?*

Write each participant's name on the outside of an empty envelope. Invite all other participants to write (anonymously) which personality type they think that person is and place it in the named envelope.

Step 3. *Who Am I?*

Before the envelope is opened, each participant is allowed one minute to describe which type they think they are. They then open their envelope to see themselves as others see them.

These exercises make a fun training session because of the interest we all have in discovering more about ourselves. You can use this technique to make your training entertaining, exciting, and intriguing.

CHAPTER 29

How to Run Powerful Meetings

As your business grows, you'll discover the benefit of using team meetings to train and lead your growing downline. Carefully planned and well-presented meetings are powerful vehicles to motivate, entertain, and inspire your team. A lively meeting is also one of the best recruiting tools ever invented for network marketing.

"FIRE" It Up

Whether it's a small group at home, a medium-size group in a local hall, or a large group in a hotel meeting room, plan a tight agenda for every meeting. Involve each of the following elements to put "FIRE" into your meetings:

F un
I nspiration
R ecognition
E ducation.

FUN

Because you're asking people to give up time they could be using for selling, prospecting, socializing, or spending with their family, make sure your meetings are enjoyable and entertaining. A lively, fun atmosphere will help ensure everyone looks forward to, and attends, the next meeting.

INSPIRATION

Team meetings are the perfect place to share success stories at different levels of achievement. Including success testimonials in every meeting is one of the best ways to share the dream, keep it alive, and inspire your downline to stretch for higher goals.

RECOGNITION

Meetings are ideal for publicly acknowledging and celebrating progress, achievements, and successes, large and small. A warning, however—don't fall into the trap of trying to encourage people by giving recognition where it is not due. Focus your recognition on those who have achieved specific targets.

EDUCATION

Make sure every meeting reinforces at least one of the six network marketing basics:

1. Product Knowledge
2. Booking Skills
3. Selling Skills
4. Recruiting Skills
5. Leadership Skills
6. Development Skills

A little instruction on each of these key topics will build strong team members and allow new leaders to emerge.

Prospects Allowed

Encourage your downline to bring a prospect to your team meetings. Why not? Your meetings are inspirational and educational gatherings where achievements are recognized, and they're fun and entertaining, too. What better way to showcase your business opportunity! The force of a group moving in one direction is irresistible, and the success of a new recruit could help encourage others to become more interested or even totally committed on the spot. Use the momentum you create to spark interest in joining or making an appointment to learn more.

The trick is to make sure your meeting leaves in a prospect's mind the thought, "I could do that."

Meetings in your own home are inexpensive, nonthreatening, and easy to organize. Plus, you have the opportunity to get to know the people in a relaxed, informal environment. Your downline and your prospects come away thinking they have just been involved in an enjoyable way to make money and to recruit.

Bigger meetings can be excellent vehicles for a credible cross-section of testimonials. Different people saying, in just a few minutes, what they have achieved with network marketing can illustrate to prospects the excitement, momentum, and potential of the business, while creating the feeling that "people just like me" are able to succeed.

Meetings are a good opportunity for you to introduce some of the successful people in your team to your prospects. Their enthusiasm will help reassure prospective recruits that they will be in good company. Inviting a company representative along to speak at a meeting where you have prospective recruits can also be a good idea. Make sure you use someone with good communication skills who will relate to your audience.

Before any meeting, share with your prospects the purpose of the meeting. When they get a proper feel for what will be expected of them and how they can learn to be a success, they'll find the opportunity hard to resist.

The Home Meeting

When you hold a meeting with a room bursting with people it's easier to generate excitement about new product releases, promotions, and upcoming events. A large room with only a sprinkling of people is a difficult environment in which to create energy or foster team spirit.

A home meeting is best because it's low-key and easy to duplicate. You don't need to decorate the room, other than a simple product display. Just provide warm, friendly hospitality and an easily followed role model. Unless there is a special occasion or special reason—maybe once or twice a year—avoid holding your meetings in hired premises such as local halls or motel or hotel conference rooms. It's better to have a crowded small room than an empty large one.

Meetings away from a home increase your overhead (one of the key benefits of a network marketing business is its low overhead), although these costs can be reduced by sharing them with your team or by charging a small entry ticket price. No-shows—a fact of life in network marketing—are more exaggerated and more obvious in a larger venue. Another significant consideration is that hiring a venue can give the wrong signal to your prospects. They need to see you are offering them a low-overhead, easily run, at-home business.

The Bigger Meeting

The time to run a bigger meeting is when you can tag it to a new product, promotional launch, celebration, or special recognition, such as a car presentation or an international trip earned.

There can be advantages in having proper staging and audiovisual support. Your company may have staged similar functions, and you can borrow their ideas and themes. However, don't even think about holding a large meeting until your business is well established. Big or small, think of every meeting as a brilliant opportunity to showcase the magic of your network marketing business.

Twelve Things to Remember

Keep it short. Keep it uncluttered. Keep it lively. Start and finish on time.

Those 14 words should be written on the back wall of every room where a meeting is held!

Use the following 12-point checklist as a memory jogger for any meeting, from the smallest at-home training session to the largest promotional event. The principles and disciplines covered in this simple checklist apply equally to all meetings. I recommend you refer back to it whenever you plan a meeting, until it becomes second nature.

1. Purpose

Start planning the meeting by defining its purpose. What do you want to achieve? Once established, stick to it. Don't be sidetracked. I have seen valuable meetings wasted when irrelevant and inappropriate enhancements are included—fashion shows, lessons in gift-wrapping, or guest speakers who are not relevant to the purpose of the meeting. And check that you have put "FIRE" into every meeting—*Fun, Inspiration, Recognition,* and *Education*.

2. Agenda

Once you have defined the purpose of your meeting, write your agenda, putting a time frame around each item. If there's too much to cover, cut back and save things for next time. Time won't stretch just because you want it to, and meetings that run over time will be a disaster for your business, as the number of attendees dwindles.

3. Venue

If you're hiring or using an unfamiliar venue, visit it and check it out beforehand. Leave nothing to chance. Will you have to bring or hire any additional equipment: sound system, music, visual aids, whiteboard, marker pens, overhead projector, video projector, video monitor, VCR, lighting, display boards, easels for posters, adhesive tape, tables for displays, or display aids such as tablecloths, balloons, and product stands?

What about special theme props? For example, a Christmas range launch will be more special with a tree, candles, decorations, cake, a glass of champagne, some inexpensive wrapped gifts, and Christmas lights and music.

Will signage be required to help your guests find the location?

Is parking inexpensive and easily accessible? Are there sufficient spaces for the numbers attending? Are any other big events booked for the same night, which might cause problems with parking, staffing, and noise control?

Check if there is easy access to the stage (especially for a presenter wearing a tight skirt).

What is the deadline for confirming final numbers?

Run through the entire program with the venue staff and use their experience to help you. Give the venue management a written brief, including a floor plan of how you want the stage, seating, and welcome and display tables laid out. Be specific in your instructions; for example, all tables to be covered and skirted, seating to be theatre or classroom style, chairs angled rather than straight to create a less formal environment.

4. INVITATIONS

Who do you want to come to the meeting? Should you arrange a guest speaker or VIP? Get invitations out on time. Include a contact telephone number and an R.S.V.P. date that suits you and the venue. Make sure you include clear details of time and location. Sometimes a simple map is helpful. Don't rely on people remembering to respond by the R.S.V.P. date. Arrange to follow up with invitees to ensure they've received their invitation and that they will be attending. If you're busy, or the meeting involves large numbers, this is a great task to delegate to others in your downline.

On the night, have a contingency plan that allows for between 20 and 50 percent of the guests not showing up. This can happen to even the most established leaders, and the best strategy is to be prepared for it.

5. CHARGING

Is a small charge needed to help with expenses? How will this be handled? If catering is included, do you sell tickets in advance or can you accept walk-ins? A small point to consider: collecting money at the door can give the wrong impression. A small charge for a raffle drawing is fine, but try to organize any other charges beforehand. People are more likely to attend if they have purchased a ticket in advance than if they can pay at the door. All venues require an estimate of numbers if catering is involved and will not reduce their charges if turnout doesn't reach expectations. Guests who are prospective distributors must never pay.

6. Participation

Go through the agenda and determine how you can involve other members of your downline in the event. The more you involve them, the quicker they learn. Give all speakers a clear brief as early as possible.

For a big meeting, include a rehearsal in your schedule to make sure everyone knows what they are doing and when. A rehearsal will build confidence and identify any problems, such as a speaker allocated 5 minutes who speaks for 15. Practice makes perfect!

7. Chairing

A well-run meeting needs a chairperson, preferably you, to ensure the meeting starts on time, introduce each of the speakers, and generally keep the program moving along.

A good introduction of a speaker includes a mention of the topic (without delivering the speech in advance) and a reference to the speaker's credentials, for example, ". . . was top in sponsoring last year." A warm, supportive introduction will make both the speaker and the audience feel relaxed.

8. Rehearsal

On the day, arrive early and carefully check everything again. Have a dress rehearsal. If you're in a big venue, practice using the microphone. Check sound levels, remembering that later, when the room is full, the audience will absorb some of the sound. Ensure you have it set loud enough and, if possible, have someone monitor the sound levels during the presentation.

If you haven't used a microphone before, the best advice is to ignore it. Be yourself, talk normally, and let the amplification system do the work for you. Let all speakers rehearse with the sound system, so they will appear relaxed and confident.

Organize and rehearse your helpers who will look after dimming and brightening the room's lighting and handling the audiovisual system.

9. SEATING

Make sure you have more than enough chairs ready for the number of guests expected. For bigger meetings, it's a good idea not to put them all out. Set up the room a few chairs short of the required number and have spare chairs close by. This way, you don't end up with the negative of empty seating. If everyone turns up, or unexpected extras arrive, it creates a buzz of excitement and energy to be putting out extra seating at the last minute.

Ask your team to arrive early, so the first guests are not entering an empty room. Be prepared for some guests to surprise you by arriving earlier than expected.

10.   WELCOME

Have upbeat music playing well in advance of expected guest arrivals, to create an exciting, warm, and welcoming atmosphere.

It's a good strategy to place your brightest, warmest people at the door to welcome guests. Whether it's a small or a large meeting, nametags are helpful.

Before the meeting starts, greet as many of the guests as you can. Be generous with tickets for door prizes that can be drawn during the meeting.

A simple sign-in sheet will help you immensely in following up. Have the guests include their name, telephone number, and the name of the person who invited them, on a guest register.

A follow-up response slip for guests to complete, which can also go into a prize drawing, works well, too. Develop your own to suit your business and make sure it includes options for a sales consultation, an opportunity to host a show or workshop, or an appointment to learn more about your business opportunity. The slip should request name and telephone number and the best time to call so your follow-up call will be at a convenient time.

11. TIMING

Stress to your key people the importance of arriving early.

Even if some guests have not arrived by the scheduled start time, always begin the meeting promptly. Those who arrive punctually deserve the courtesy of a meeting that starts on time. Latecomers know they are late and will expect to miss the beginning.

Once you start, keep the meeting moving along and always finish on time. A discreet signal, or cue from the rear of the room, can be helpful to keep overly verbose speakers on course. This is where rehearsals help.

If your audience leaves wanting more, you've had a successful meeting. This means they will respond positively to your next meeting invitation.

12. THANK YOU

Don't forget to recognize and thank all who contributed to the meeting—from the audience who gave up their time to be there to the guest speakers and the people behind the scenes whose work helped ensure the meeting's success. Small gifts are always appreciated.

PART EIGHT

The Magic

in You

CHAPTER 30

Test Your Leadership Skills

A million-dollar network marketing business is built on strong leadership. When you strengthen your leadership skills, you strengthen your business.

The Qualities of Leadership

Use this list of the key qualities of a successful leader to measure your progress toward excellence in L E A D E R S H I P.

L eading by example
E nergy
A dding value
D iscipline
E mpowerment
R ecognition
S kills
H onesty
I ndependence
P erseverance

LEADING BY EXAMPLE

Are you the best seller, best recruiter, and best trainer in your team? Do you work hard, keeping a calm and happy demeanor, to set an example for others to duplicate? Ask yourself, "If I cloned myself, how effective would my organization be?"

To be a successful leader, you must be able to recognize your own strengths and weaknesses, as these will filter down through your organization. While you constantly seek to improve, learn, and grow, always acknowledge your strengths. Women are often slow to do this. Use all your strengths, abilities, and skills to enhance your business.

You'll find, as a leader, it's what you do, not what you say that counts.

ENERGY

This is a high-energy business. It's an adventure, never certain but always exciting. Your energy will act as an irresistible magnet to others. Are you generating enough energy to build and maintain momentum?

ADDING VALUE

Seek to add value to everyone and everything you touch and you'll not only be seen as an excellent leader, you'll also build outstanding loyalty and increased business. Give added value to your customers by delivering better service than they expect. Do the same with your downline by selflessly and generously sharing your knowledge, skills, and experience.

DISCIPLINE

It's not how hard you work but the way you work that makes the difference. Good leaders resist the temptation to do what's easiest at the expense of what's a priority. They have also learned the discipline of letting go of the things that can prevent them achieving their goals. Have you learned the self-discipline of delegating tasks, allowing others to learn by doing, and focusing on the key success factors that will drive your business?

EMPOWERMENT

Are you empowering yourself and others? Self-empowerment comes from developing the ability to recognize the things you're doing or not doing that cause a situation you're not happy with and then taking responsibility for doing something about it. You empower other people and help them grow by giving them responsibility for their own actions. When they know you believe in their abilities and see you step aside, you'll see the power of leadership in action.

RECOGNITION

Never underestimate the difference you can make by being generous with appropriate praise and recognition. Recognition is a powerful tool that can result in enhanced self-esteem and improved performance.

Do you celebrate your achievements and those of your downline (both large and small)?

Do you look for reasons to praise and use praise often?

Do you set goals for your team that stretch them, then recognize their growth in achieving them? No single action shows people how important they are to you better than seeking their assistance and advice.

SKILLS

Are you developing your skills, constantly learning more about your products and the business? Are you keeping up with the new technologies? Are you encouraging your team to continue their education? The more skills you have, the more you can lead others.

HONESTY

Do you set an immaculate example to your downline? Always be honest in all matters. Pay your bills on time. Keep proper records. Run your business ethically. Never compete with your distributors or let them down. In a business where the highest rewards come to those who give the most to others, the example you set will have far-reaching effects.

INDEPENDENCE

Do you take responsibility for the success of your business, the direction you take it, and the income you make from it? A good leader is not at the mercy of people and events around them. When we take individual responsibility, we take control. There is great freedom in relinquishing the belief that others control our lives. Treasure your independence.

PERSEVERANCE

Are you able to work long hours and focus on the priorities that build your business?

Do you take care not to be distracted or burdened by things that may or may not come about. Mark Twain put it so well when he said, "I've had some terrible times in my life, some of which actually happened."

There's a lot to be learned from history's great leaders. Britain's Sir Winston Churchill reportedly returned to his old school and gave the young pupils advice on leadership and how to run their lives. His wisdom was encapsulated in just nine words: "Never give in. Never give in. Never give in."

Consistent, persistent effort will always win out.

The most successful leaders know that leadership is a privilege, not a right, a chance to serve others and help them develop their true potential.

Aim for 10 out of 10 in L E A D E R S H I P and you're guaranteed success in network marketing and in your personal life, too.

Your 12-Point Leadership Checklist

There comes a time for all of us when we need a little extra motivation. This 12-point checklist will remind you how to do it. Once you have mastered all 12 points for yourself and made them a regular part of your daily life, it's easy to instill them in your downline.

MOTIVATING YOURSELF
What you do for yourself

1. Keep a positive outlook. When you experience challenges, you'll find optimism works wonders.
2. Believe in yourself. Guess what—there's no one else in the world quite like you! Remind yourself, "If it's going to be, it's up to me."
3. Set yourself meaningful and achievable goals and keep measuring your success.
4. Develop and follow an action plan.
5. Find ways to enjoy what you're doing.
6. Keep your enthusiasm levels high. Celebrate your achievements!
7. Be kind to yourself. Self-criticism will lead you nowhere.
8. Move on from your mistakes. Learn from them and grow.
9. Avoid negative people. Know when to cut loose and move away. Surround yourself with successful, positive people.
10. Never stop learning.
11. Know that you will succeed.
12. Set yourself new challenges.

MOTIVATING OTHERS
What you do for others

1. Let your positive outlook be infectious. Spread it around.
2. Tell and show your downline you believe in them.
3. Work to set meaningful, measurable, and achievable goals.
4. Develop an action plan with them and help them stick to it.
5. Keep it fun for them.
6. Acknowledge and recognize their achievements, privately and publicly.
7. Never criticize. Instead, commend their achievements, make recommendations, and lead by example.
8. Don't worry about their mistakes, they need to make them. Your role is to help them learn by doing.
9. Overcome any negativity with action plans, tips, training, new ideas.
10. Show them, by example, how to duplicate themselves.
11. Keep dreams alive by constantly reinforcing the big picture.
12. Encourage them to keep setting challenges for themselves.

CHAPTER 31

Success Is in
Your Own Hands

As I said in the beginning, this book is not about the successes other people are enjoying, it's about you. Now that you have the knowledge and the tools to make your first million in network marketing, your success lies in practicing, perfecting, and sharing your skills.

Some Final Advice

You can become a millionaire. Countless numbers of people around the world are doing it in network marketing every day. They started just like you, with no customers and no downline. They did it by using skills and ideas outlined in this book.

Persevere and you will find these skills and ideas work.

When you practice your skills, do it with generosity of spirit. Focus on giving, not getting, and give cheerfully. You'll find the more you give in network marketing (as in life), magically, the more you get.

Share your knowledge.

Lead by example. Don't expect others to do what you're not doing yourself.

Know that anything can be achieved, when it's achieved in small steps. Sometimes, though, you'll need the courage it takes to make a great leap. You can't cross a chasm in two small jumps.

Your role as a leader is to light the path for others to follow.

Keep everyone's dreams alive, as well as your own. Dream big, dream strong, and dream with your eyes open. The brightest flame is the hardest to extinguish.

When you're listening, listen hard. Not just to what others are saying, but to why they are saying it.

Just about everything worthwhile we achieve in life comes from within, not from outside influences. Believe in yourself, in your products, and in your network marketing business.

Teach yourself to speak slowly but think quickly.

Know that life is too short to let a little dispute injure a good friendship.

When you make a mistake, act immediately to acknowledge and correct it. Know that you will make mistakes. It's the only way to learn.

Sometimes not getting what you want can be a wonderful stroke of luck.

Remain open to change, because the world is constantly changing, but hold onto your values.

Have faith in the ability of the people you recruit. And constantly let them know it.

Beyond all else, relax and have fun! It's your business, your life, and you are in control.

Making your first million in network marketing will take as long as it takes. Don't allow yourself to become downhearted, discouraged, or depressed. And don't leave the business. Believe you can do it, keep focused, and keep working until you achieve the goals you have set yourself.

I wish you every success with your business, the same success that's enjoyed by millions of people in network marketing around the world. I know if you use the information detailed in this book, your success can be as big as your dreams.

Finally, never underestimate your power to change lives. You'll discover that while you're changing other people, you're changing yourself as well.

In closing, I would like to share with you these few lines, in the hope that they will help you keep your perspective as you grow from success to success, using network marketing magic to make your first million.

I dream a dream to change the world
But don't know where to start.
I am just one person,
One tiny little part.
They told me I could do it
If only I could see
There is a way to change the world;
It starts by changing me.

To book Mary Christensen as a keynote speaker for your conference or seminar, call (403) 630-5600, write to her at marychristensenmlm @hotmail.com or visit her Web site: *www.marychristensen.com*

Share Your Success Story

Are you willing to be a role model, to share your story and help inspire others to achieve success? Mary Christensen is looking for network marketing millionaires to profile in her forthcoming book on network marketing role models. For more information, e-mail her at *marychristensenmlm@hotmail.com* or check out her Web site: *www.marychristensen.com*.

Members of the United States Direct Selling Association

The following list was current at time of publication. For more up-to-date information, check with the Direct Selling Association, 1275 Pennsylvania Ave NW, Suite 800, Washington, DC 20004, USA. Tel: (202) 347-8866. e-mail: *info@dsa.org*

Achievers Unlimited, Inc.
Nutritional products
(561) 835-3777

Act II Jewelry, Inc.—Lady Remington
Jewelry
(708) 860-3323

Advocare International
Weight management and skincare products
(214) 831-1033

AIM U.S.A.
Nutritional products
(800) 456-2462

Aloette
Skincare, cosmetics, fragrances
(800)-ALOETTE

AMC Corporation
Cookware
(203) 363-0331

American Communications Network, Inc. (ACN, Inc.)
Long-distance services, debit calling cards, pay phones
(810) 528-2500

Amway Corporation
Homecare, nutritional, personal care, and commercial products/services
(616) 787-6000

Arbonne International, Inc.
Skincare, cosmetics, nutritional
products
(949) 770-2610

Art Finds International
Art
(317) 248-2666

Artistic Impressions Inc.
Art
(630) 916-0050

Assured Nutrition Plus
Nutritional and weight management products
(937) 548-7713

Avon Products, Inc.
Cosmetics, decorative accessories,
giftware, jewelry, skincare,
toys/games, and nutritional
products
(800) FOR-AVON

BeautiControl Cosmetics, Inc.
Cosmetics, skincare, nutritional
products, image services
(800) BEAUTI-I

Big Planet
Internet products, long-distance
service
(800) 211-6300

Body Wise International
Nutritional products
(800) 830-9596

Carico International, Inc.
Cookware, water treatment systems, juice extractor, china, crystal,
cutlery, tableware, air filters
(800) 422-7426

Changes International, Inc.
Nutritional products
(800) 933-7424

Charmelle
Jewelry
(800) 846-5393

Colesce Couture, Inc.
Lingerie and sleepwear
(214) 631-4860

Conklin Company, Inc.
Personal and homecare products
(800) 888-8838

Cookin' The American Way
(Division of House of Lloyd)
Cookware
(800) 733-2465

**The Country Peddlers & Company
of America, Inc.**
Decorative accessories
(800) 873-3537

Creative Memories
Photo albums and photo album
supplies
(800) 468-9335

Cutco/Vector Corporation
Cutlery
(800) 828-0448

Discovery Toys
Toys/games, books, childcare products, educational materials, videos
(800) 426-4777

DK Family Learning
Books and videos
(407) 857-5463

Doncaster
Clothing and fashion accessories
(800) 669-3662

DS-Max U.S.A., Inc.
Books, business products,
plants/foliage, toys/games, giftware, and house- and kitchenwares
(714) 587-9207

Dudley Products, Inc.
Cosmetics, fragrances, skincare,
and hair care
(336) 993-8800

Eagle Distributing Company
Fire alarms and extinguishers
(800) 825-5880

Electrolux Corporation
Vacuum cleaners and homecare
products
(800) 243-9078

Enrich International
Skincare and health/fitness
products
(801) 226-2224

**Essentially Yours Industries
Corporation**
Nutritional products, weight management products
(604) 596-9766

Eventus International, Inc.
Nutritional products
(800) 943-8085

Excel Communications, Inc.
Long-distance service
(800) 875-9235

For You, Inc.
Skincare, self-improvement
programs
(843) 756-9000

Freelife International
Nutrition products, skincare
(800) 882-7240

The Fuller Brush Company
Homecare products, house- and
kitchenwares, personal care
products
(316) 792-1711

Golden Neo-Life Diamite International
Nutritional products, homecare products, skincare, water treatment systems, weight management products
(510) 651-0405

Golden Pride International
Nutritional, weight management, health/fitness products, house- and kitchenwares, water treatment systems, food/beverage products, skincare
(561) 640-5700

The Good Nature Company
Bird feeding products, garden accessories
(248) 628-4103

Henn Workshops
Decorative accessories
(330) 824-2575

Herbalife International
Weight management products, nutritional products, personal care products, and fragrances
(310) 410-9600

Highlights-Jigsaw Toy Factory, Ltd.
Educational materials, toys/games, books
(614) 324-7902

Holbrook Cottage, Inc.
Home accessories, gifts, and gourmet foods
(914) 944-0734

Home & Garden Party, Inc.
Pottery, art, and decorative accessories
(800) 700-7873

Home Interiors & Gifts, Inc.
Giftware and decorative accessories
(972) 386-1000

The Homemaker's Idea Co. (Wicker World Enterprises)
Decorative accessories
(800) 800-5452

House Of Lloyd, Inc.
Christmas items, giftware, decorative accessories, and toys/games
(800) 733-2465

Hsin Ten Enterprise USA, Inc.
Health/fitness products
(631) 777-8883

Hy Cite Corporation
Cookware, crystal/china, cutlery, air purification and water treatment systems
(608) 663-0600

Integris International, Inc.
Nutritional products
(972) 929-7307

Interstate Engineering
Vacuum cleaners
(714) 758-5011

Jafra Cosmetics International, Inc.
Skincare, cosmetics, and fragrances
(805) 449-3000

Jeunique International, Inc.
Cosmetics, lingerie/sleepwear,
nutritional products, and skincare
(909) 598-8598

Kelly's Kids, Inc.
Children's clothing
(800) 837-2066

Kids Only Clothing Club
Clothing
(403) 252-9667

The Kirby Company
Vacuum cleaners
(216) 228-2400

Kitchen Fair (Regal Ware, Inc.)
Cookware, decorative accessories,
house- and kitchenwares
(501) 982-0555

Learning Wonders
Educational materials
(800) 537-7227

Legacy USA, Inc.
Nutritional products
(407) 951-8815

LifeScience Technologies, Ltd
Nutritional products, personal care
products, telecommunications
services, prepaid calling cards,
long-distance service
(800) 522-8000

The Longaberger Company
Decorative accessories, house- and
kitchenwares
(614) 754-5000

Longevity Network, Ltd.
Nutritional products, skincare, hair
care, personal care products
(800) 242-1000

Magnus Enterprises, Inc.
Nutritional products, cosmetics
(310) 532-8440

Mannatech, Inc.
Nutritional products
(888) 346-4636

Market America, Inc.
Personal care products, nutritional
products, homecare products, auto-
care products, and photography
(910) 605-0040

Mary Kay Cosmetics, Inc.
Cosmetics and skincare products
(800) 627-9529

Melaleuca, Inc.
Nutritional products, personal care
products, homecare products
(208) 522-0700

Millennium Direct Marketing, Inc.
Nutritional products, skincare

Morinda, Inc.
Nutritional products, Noni juice
(801) 431-6000

**Muscle Dynamics
Fitness Network, Inc.**
Health/fitness, nutrition, and
weight management products
(310) 715-8036

The Nationwide Companies
Benefits packages, jewelry, nutritional products, telecommunications, automobiles
(800) 273-2517

Nature's Own
Skincare, nutritional products,
health/fitness products
(203) 380-8900

NestFamily.com
Bible videotapes, audiotapes,
educational materials
(888) 777-NEST

Nature's Sunshine Products, Inc.
Cookware, nutritional products,
skincare, and water treatment
systems
(801) 342-4300

New Image International
Weight management and nutrition
(502) 867-1895

New Vision International, Inc.
Nutritional products, personal
care products, skincare, sports
supplements, weight management
products
(800) 646-3725

Nikken, Inc.
Nutritional and bedding products
(714) 789-2000

Noevir USA, Inc.
Cosmetics, skincare, and nutrition
(800) 872-8817

NSA
Air filters, water treatment, educational materials, and nutritional
products
(901) 366-9288

Nu Skin International, Inc.
Hair care, nutritional products, and
skincare items
(801) 345-1000

NuMED USA, Inc.
Health/fitness products, nutritional
products
(727) 524-3227

NutraBiotics Research Labs, Inc.
Nutritional products
(516) 942-3462

Nutri-Metics North America
Skincare, homecare products, nutritional products
(403) 279-2595

Nutrition For Life International, Inc.
Nutrition, weight management,
skincare, long-distance service,
Internet advertising services, and
homeopathics
(713) 460-1976

Oriflame U.S.A.
Skincare, cosmetics, fragrances,
and nutritional products
(800) 959-0699

Oxyfresh Worldwide, Inc.
Dental hygiene, skincare and personal care, nutritional products,
animal care, and homecare
(509) 924-4999

The Pampered Chef, Ltd.
House-, kitchen-, and cookware
(800) 266-5562 (USA only)
(800) 342-2433 (Canada only)

Partylite Gifts, Inc.
Candles, candle accessories
(508) 830-3100

Petra Fashions, Inc.
Lingerie/sleepwear
(978) 777-5853

**Pharmanex, Inc. (A division
of Nu Skin Enterprises)**
Nutritional products, weight management products
(888) PHARMANEX

Pola U.S.A., Inc.
Cosmetics, fragrances, hair care,
and skincare products
(310) 527-9696

Premier Designs, Inc.
Jewelry
(800) 484-7378

Primerica Financial Services
Financial/investment services and
insurance
(770) 381-1000

Princess House, Inc.
Decorative accessories,
crystal/china, and jewelry
(800) 622-0039

Providence House, LLC
Catholic books and gifts
(803) 802-4360

Rachael International, Inc.
Skincare, hair care, cosmetics,
nutritional products
(407) 814-0222

Regal Ware, Inc.
Cookware, cutlery, tableware, and
water treatment systems
(262) 626-2121

Reliv' International, Inc.
Nutritional products, personal care
products
(636) 537-9715

Rena-Ware Distributors, Inc.
Cookware
(206) 881-6171

Rexair, Inc.
Vacuum cleaners, homecare
products
(248) 643-7222

Rexall Showcase International
Nutrition, water treatment, personal
care, and health/fitness products
(561) 994-2090

Rich Plan Corporation
Food/beverage products and home
appliances
(800) 662-3663

Saladmaster, Inc. (Regal Ware, Inc.)
Cookware and tableware
(817) 633-3555

Seaborne, Inc.
Nutritional products
(877) 738-0990

Shaklee Corporation
Nutritional products, personal care
products, homecare products, and
water treatment systems
(415) 954-3000

Shaperite
Weight management and personal
care products
(888) 742-7374

The Southwestern Company
Books and educational materials
(615) 391-2500

Sportron International, Inc.
Nutrition, skincare, weight management products, and homecare
(972) 509-1234

Stampin' Up
Rubber Stamps
(800)-STAMP UP

Stanley Home Products
Homecare products, personal care
products, wellness products
(800) 628-9032

The Story Teller
Books, educational materials, toys,
games, and cassettes
(801) 423-2560

Sunrider International
Nutritional products, skincare, personal care products, cosmetics, and homecare products
(310) 781-3808

SupraLife
Nutritional products, skincare, hair care, oral hygiene
(800) 359-3245

Symmetry Corporation
Nutrition products, and weight management products
(408) 942-7700

Tarrah
Skincare products
(561) 640-5700

Taste of Gourmet
Food/beverage products
(662) 887-2522

Tomorrow's Treasures, Inc.
Home photography workshops, photo lab services, enlargements, processing, personalized photo gift items, photo display items
(800) 899-5656

Totally Tropical Interiors Ltd.
Plants/foliage, and decorative accessories
(403) 291-9366

Trek Alliance, Inc.
Weight management products, nutritional products, and skincare
(775) 833-TREK

Tupperware Corporation
House and kitchenware, and toys/games
(407) 847-3111

UCC Total Home
Group Buying Service
(219) 736-1100

U.S. Safety & Engineering Corporation
Security systems/devices
(916) 482-8888

Usana, Inc.
Nutritional products and skincare
(801) 954-7100

Usborne Books At Home
Books
(800) 475-4522

Vantel Pearls In The Oyster
Pearls and jewelry
(508) 698 2220

Vita Craft Corporation
Cookware, crystal/china, cutlery, tableware, and water treatment
(913) 631-6265

Viva Life Science, Inc.
Nutrition, skincare, fitness, and
weight management products
(800) 243-VIVA

Viviane Woodward Industries, Inc.
Skincare, cosmetics, fragrances
(800) 423-3600

Vorwerk USA Company, L.P.
Food preparation appliance,
floor care
(407) 772-2222

Watkins Incorporated
Nutritional products, personal care
products, food/beverage products,
and homecare products
(507) 457-3300

Weekender USA, Inc.
Clothing
(847) 465-1666

The West Bend Company
Cookware and water treatment
systems
(262) 334-2311

Wicker Plus, Ltd.
Decorative accessories
(262) 255-7377

Willow Home & Garden
Home Accessories, garden accessories
(313) 792-1503

World Book, Inc.
Encyclopedias and educational
materials
(800) WORLDBK

Youngevity, Inc.
Nutritional products
(800) 439-6864

Yves Rocher Direct Selling
Beauty care
(888) 909-0771

Members of the World Federation of Direct Selling Associations (WFDSA)

The following list was current at time of publication. For more up-to-date information, check with the World Federation of Direct Selling Associations, 1275 Pennsylvania Ave NW, Washington, DC 20004, USA. Tel: (202) 347-8866. E-mail: *info@wfdsa.org*

ARGENTINA
Camara Agentine De Venta Directas
(C.A.V.E.D.I)
Florida 878, 8th Floor,
Office 30th,
10005 Buenos Aires,
Argentina
Tel: (54) 1-311-9713
Fax: (54) 1-311-315-2940
E-mail:
 jmendez@betterware.com.ar
Jorge Mendez

AUSTRALIA
Direct Selling Association of Australia
450 North Road
Langwarrin, Victoria 3910
Australia
Tel: (61) 3-9785-6233
Tel: (61) 3-9785-6244
Fax: (61) 3-9785-6255
E-mail: *dsaa@dsaa.asn.au*
Web site: *www.dsaa.asn.au*
John Fulton

AUSTRIA
Arbeitsgruppe Directvertrieb
"Zu Hause beraten gut gekauft"
Handelsverband
AlserstraBe45 A
1080 Vienna
Austria
Tel: (43) 1-406-22-36
Fax: (43) 1-408-64-81
Hildegard Fischer

BELGIUM
Direct Selling Association of Belgium
Rue Saint Bernard, 60
B-1060 Brussels
Belgium
Tel: (32) 2-539-3060
Fax: (32) 9-251-3818
E-mail: *krp@fedis.be*
Kristien Pollars

BRAZIL
DOMUS Assacia Brasileira de Empresas
de Vendes Directas
Rua Tabapua, 649 Conj 33
04533-012 Sao Paulo,
SP Brazil
Tel: (55) 1-822-5316
Fax: (55) 1-822-5316
E-mail: *domus@domus.org.br*
Web site: *www.domus.org.br*
Lidia Dias

CANADA
Direct Sellers Association 180 Attwell
Drive
Suite 250
Etobicoke, Ontario
Canada M9W 6A9
Tel: (1) 416-679-8555
Fax: (1) 416-679-1568
E-mail: *information@dsa.org*
Web site: *www.dsa.ca*
Paul Thériault

CHILE
Camara de Venta Directa de Chile, A.G.
Mireflores 222, Piso 24
Santiago
Chile
Tel: (56) 2-365-7200
Fax: (56) 2-633-1980
E-mail: *asilva@carey.cl*
Alfonso Silva

COLOMBIA
ACOVEDI DSA of Colombia
Calle 95 No. 13-55
Oficina 203
Santafe De Bogota
Colombia
Tel: (571) 621-4056
Fax: (571) 621-4042
E-mail: *acovedi@impsat.net.co*
Guillermo Hernandez Gartner

COSTA RICA
Camara Costarricense De Empresas De
Venta Directa (DSA of Costa Rica)
PO Box 8298
San Costa Rica Jose, 1000
Tel: (506) 256-7557
Fax: (506) 256-0363
E-mail: *oriflame@racsa.co.cr*
Wilbert Rosales Gomez

CZECH REPUBLIC
Direct Selling Association of the Czech
Republic
C/O Amway CR
Nad Kazankou 29
170 00 Praha 7
Czech Republic
Tel: (42) 2-830-17-120
Fax: (42) 2-854-21-00
E-mail: *jan_stransky@amway.com*
Jan Stransky

DENMARK
Direkte Salgs Foreningen (DSF)
C/O Tupperware Scandinavia A/S
Sejrogade 9
DK-2100 Copenhagen 0
Denmark
Tel: (45) 39-27-23-24
Fax: (45) 39-27-26-64
E-mail:
  ssorenson@tupperware.dk
Soren Sorenson

EL SALVADOR
Directorio Associacion
Salvandorena De Venta Directa C/O
Productos Avon
Boulevard Santa Elena Y,
CalleConchagua
Colonia Santa Elena
Antiguo Cuscatlan
El Salvador
Tel: (503) 289-4343
Fax: (503) 289-4317
E-mail:
  Rodrigo.Delgado@avon.com
Rodrigo Delgado

FINLAND
Suomen Suoramarkkinointiliitto ry
Lonnrotinkatu 11 A
00120 Helsinki
Finland
Tel: (358) 9 6121 070
Fax: (358) 9 6121 039
E-mail: *sakke@ssml.fdma.fi*
Web site: *www.ssml-fdma.fi*
Sakari Virtanen

FRANCE
Syndicat de la Vente Directe
8, Place D'Iena
75783 Paris Cedex 16
France
Tel: (33) 01-4434-68-60
Fax: (33) 01-47-55-17-83
E-mail: *svd@club_Internet.Fr*
Web site: *www.usernet.org/svd*
Philippe Dailey

GERMANY
Arbeitskreis 'Gut Beraten - Zu Hause
Gekauft' E.V.
Klugstr. 53
80638 Munich
Germany
Tel: (49) 89-154=634
Fax: (49) 89=157=6684
E-mail: *info@ak-gutberaten.de*
Wolfgang Bohle

GREECE
Greek Union of Direct Selling Companies
61b Apostolou Pavlou Str.
Thissio-118 51 Athens
Greece
Tel: (30) 1-3421-579
Fax: (30) 1-3421-913
Stavros Efremides

GUATEMALA
Asociacion Guatemalteca de Vantas
Directas
C/O Avon Cosmeticos
Calzada Roosevelt 11-08
Zona 2 De Mixco
Guatemala City, Guatemala
Tel: (502) 594 8056
Tel: (502) 594 6425
Fax: (502) 594 3058
E-mail:
   Miguel.Salbitano@avon.com
Miguel Salbitano

HONDURAS
Asociacion Hondurena De Empresas
Venta Directa
C/O Productos Avon, S.A.
8 Avenida S.O., 7 Y 8
Calle #61
San Pedro Sula
Honduras
Tel: (504) 552-6118
Fax: (504) 557-3883
E-mail:
   Stephen.Smith@avon.com
Stephen Smith

HONG KONG
The Direct Selling Association of Hong
Kong, Ltd.
PO Box 54445, North Point Post Office
Hong Kong
Tel: (852) 2969-633
Tel: (852) 2969-6311
Fax: (852) 2807-3920
E-mail:
   Angela_Keung@amway.com
Angela Keung

HUNGARY
Kozvetlen Ertekesitok Svovetsege
Erzsebet kiralyne etja 1/C
B epulet 1.Emelet 114
1146 Budapest.
Tel/Fax: (36) 1-344-49-51
Mobile tel: (36) 30-517-188
Eva Rajki

INDIA
Indian Direct Selling Association
C/O Sangeet Shyamala Cultural Institute
A-12, Opposite A-11/6,
Vasant Vihar
New Delhi 1100 048
India
Tel/Fax: (91) 11-614-1005
Email: *idsa.del@rmy.sprintrpg.*
   ems.vsnl.net.in
Koyalgeet Kaur Hanjra

INDONESIA
Indonesian Direct Selling Association
C/O Avon Indon, 208 Cilandek
Commercial Jl,
Raya KKO Cilandak
Jakarta, 12560
Indonesia
Tel: (62) 21-780-1200
Fax: (62) 21-780-1712
E-mail:
   helmy.attamimi@avon.com
Helmy Attamimi

IRELAND
Direct Selling Association of Ireland
Carmichael House Business Centre
60 Lower Baggot Street
Dublin 2 Ireland
Tel: (353) 1-662-7258
Fax: (353) 1-676-2447
E-mail: *info@cmh.ie*
Web site:
 www.usernet.org/dsa-ireland
Peter Grala

ISRAEL
Direct Selling Association of Israel
7 Hashachaf Street
PO Box 1155
Caesarea, 38900
Israel
Tel: (972) 6-636-3393
Fax: (972) 6-626-4834
Joseph Shlain

ITALY
Associazione Nazionale Vendite Dirette
Servizio
Consumatori (AVEDISCO)
Viale Andrea Doria 8
Milano MI, I-20124
Italy
Tel: (392) 670-2744
Fax: (392) 670-5141
E-mail: *avedisco@tin.it*
Web site:
 www.usernet.org/avedisco
Giorgio Giulliani

JAPAN
Japan Direct Selling Association
Hosoi Bulding, 4-1
Yotsuya
Shinjuku-ku
Tokyo 160
Japan
Tel: (81) 33-357-6531
Fax: (81) 33-357-6585
E-mail: *jdsa@mbb.nifty.ne_jp*
Web site: *www.jdsa.or.jp*
Shoji Takaya

KOREA
Korean Direct Selling Association Room
404, Salvation Army Office
58-1
1-Ga, Shinmun-Ro,
Chongro-Gu
Seoul
Korea
Tel: (82) 02-733-8647
Fax: (82) 02-722-4244
Ki-Jung Bae

MALAYSIA
Direct Selling Association-Malaysia
30A 1st Floor, Jalan SS
15/8 Lock Bag 20
P.O. Subang Jaya, 47500
Subang Jaya
Selangor Darul Ehsan
Malaysia
Tel: (60) 3-734-6921
Fax: (60) 3-735-1264
E-mail: *dsamsk@tm.net.my*
Christina Ng

MEXICO
Associacion Mexicana de Ventas Directas
Insurgentes Sur 1216-503
Co. Del Valle
Mexico, D.F., 03100
Mexico
Tel: (525) 575-47-89
Fax: (525) 575-82-37
E-mail:
 amvd@mail.Internet.com.mx
Web site: *www.amvd.org.mx*
Guillermo Sanchez de Anda

NETHERLANDS
Vereniging Direkte Verkoop
Reitseplein 1
PO Box 90154
5000 LG Tilburg
Netherlands
Tel: (31) 013-594-4300
Fax: (31) 013-594-4747
E-mail: *vdv@vsam.spaendonck.nl*
Web site: *www.spaendonck.nl*
Godewinus P. van den Hurk

NEW ZEALAND
Direct Selling Association of New
Zealand, Inc.
Level 2, 159 Khyber Pass Road
Private Bag 92-066
Auckland, New Zealand
Tel: (64) 9-367-0913
Mobile: (64) 21-649 900
Fax: (64) 9-367-0914
E-mail: *wyllie@dsanz.co.nz*
Web site: *www.dsanz.co.nz*
Garth Wyllie

NORWAY
Direktesalgsforbundet
C/o Oriflame Norge A/S
Postboks 95 Okern
N-0508 Oslo
Norway
Tel: (47) 22-64-35-50
Fax: (47) 22-64-94-33
E-mail: *malke@online.no*
Nils Jakob Moen

PANAMA
Direct Selling Association of
Panama
C/O Avon Cosmeticos
Calzada Roosevelt 11-08
Zona 2 De Mixco
Guatemala City
Guatemala
Tel: (502) 594-8056
Tel: (502) 594-6425
Fax: (502) 594-3058
E-mail:
   Mariela.Delvalle@avon.com
Mariela Delvalle

PERU
Associacion Peruana DeEmpresas De
Venta Directa
C/o Avon Productos
Av. Guardia Peruana
Pasaje Vesta No. 183
La Campina, Chorrillos
Peru
Tel: (511) 467-7454
Fax: (511) 467-4106
E-mail: *Jesus.Nunez@avon.com*
Jesus Nunez

THE PHILIPPINES
Direct Selling Association of the
Philippines
C/O Avon, 2nd Floor,
Fortune Building
160 Legaspi St, Legaspi Village
Makati, Metro Manila
The Philippines
Tel: (63) 2-891-3344
Fax: (63) 2-891-3385
Jose Mari Franco

POLAND
Polskie Stowarzyszenie Sprzedazy
Bezposredniej
C/O AMC Polska
U1. Polna 50, IV
00-644 Warsaw
Poland
Tel: (48) 22-825-9783
Fax: (48) 22-825-5450
E-mail: *pssb@polbox.pl*
Web site: *www.pssb.polbox.pl/czl pssb.html*
Kurt Bressler

PORTUGAL
Associacao de Empresas de Venda Directa
C/O Avon Portugal
Av. Fontes Pereira de Melo 14-5
1050 Lisbon
Portugal
Tel: (351) 1-316-5100
Tel: (351) 1-316-5120
E-mail: *rui.rodrigues@avon.com*
Rui Rodrigues

RUSSIA
Direct Selling Association of Russia
C/O Avon Beauty Products-Russia
Ulansky Per., 4, Bld. 1
Moscow, 101000
Russia
Tel: 095-7923611
Fax: 095-7923641
John Law

SINGAPORE
Direct Selling Association of Singapore
Newton PO Box 0127
Singapore 912205
Singapore
Tel: (65) 293-0055
Fax: (65) 352-9093
Benjamin Tan

SLOVENIA
The Direct Selling Association of Slovenia
C/O Aktiva Cosmetics
D.O.O
Dunajska 156 Ljubljana
Slovenia
Tel: (386) 61-168-8115
Fax: (386) 61-168-8294
E-mail: *Bostjan.Erzen@anova.net*
Bostjan Erzen

SOUTH AFRICA
Direct Selling Association of South Africa
C/O Johannesburg Chamber of Commerce
Private Bag 34
Auckland Park 2006
South Africa
Tel: (27) 11-726-5300
Fax: (27) 11-726-8421
E-mail: *prpartner@yebo.co.za*
Jean McKenzie

SPAIN
Asociacion de Empresas de Venta Directa
Calle Aragon, 210
7th Floor, Suite 5
08011 Barcelona
Spain
Tel: (34) 93-451-56-17
Fax: (34) 93-451-59-42
E-mail: *J.Turro@avd.es*
Web site: *www.avd.es*
Juan Turro

SWEDEN
Direkthandelforetagens Forening
Johanneslustgatan 1
S-212 28 Malmo
Sweden
Tel: (46) 40-29-43-70
Fax: (46) 40-29-43-82
E-mail: *kansliet@dff.m.se*
Web site: *www.dff.m.se*
Vilmar Pohjanen

SWITZERLAND
Verband der
  Direcktverkaufsfirmen
Elisabethenanlage 7
Postfach 3257
Ch-4002 Basel
Switzerland
Tel: (41) 61-22-19-19
Fax: (41) 61-22-85-02
E-mail: *stegerk@hinderling.ch*
Hans Georg Hinderling

TAIWAN
Taiwan Direct Selling Association
15/F No. 97, Tun-Hwa S. Road,
Sect. 2
Taipei, Taiwan
Tel: (886) 22-775-8500
Fax: (886) 22-707-5999
E-mail: *Lfranc@nuskin.net*
Web site: *www.dsa.com.tw*
Francisco Liu

THAILAND
The Thai Direct Selling Association
C/O Avon Thailand
1765 Ramkamhaeng Road
Huamark, Bangkapi
Bangkok
Thailand
Tel: (66) 2314-1415
Fax: (66) 2319-2053
E-mail:
  Sittisak.Haputpong@avon.com
Sittisak Haputpong

TURKEY
Dogrudan Satis Dernegi
(DSA of Turkey)
Tunus Cad. 66
Kavakhdere
Ankara, 06680
Turkey
Tel: (90) 312-468-7764
Fax: (90) 312-468-7897
E-mail: *ibrahimy@alke.com.tr*
Ibrahim Yogurtcuoglu

UNITED KINGDOM
The Direct Selling Association, Ltd.
Unit 6, Carriage Hall
29 Floral Street
London, WC2E 9DP
England
Tel: (44) 171-497-1234
Fax: (44) 171-497-3144
Email: *ukdsa@globalnet.co.uk*
Web site: *www.dsa.org.uk*
Richard Berry

UNITED STATES
The Direct Selling Association
1666 K Street, N.W.
Suite 1010
Washington, DC 20006
United States of America
Tel: (202) 293-5760
Fax: (202) 463-4569
E-mail: *info@dsa.org*
Web site: *www.dsa.org*
Neil H. Offen

URUGUAY
Camara de Empresas de Servicio Directo
Isabela 3264 (12.000)
Montevideo
Uruguay
Tel: (598) 2-215-2121
Fax: (598) 2-216-2136
E-mail: *asiecola@nuvo.com.uy*
Abel Sade

VENEZUELA
Direct Selling Association of Venezuela -
CEVEDIR
C/O Avon
Intercommunal Guarenas
Quatire, Urb. El Marquez Edo.
Miranda
Venezuela
Tel: (58) 36-401-501
Fax: (58) 36-401-001
E-mail:
   Rufino.Hernandez@avon.com
Rufino Hernandez

EUROPE
FEDSA
Federation of European Direct Selling
Association
14 Avenue Do Terrueren (Bte 1)
B-1040 Brussels
Belgium
Tel: (32) 2-736-1014
Fax: (32) 2-736-3497
E-mail: *fedsa@fedsa.be*
Web site: *www.fedsa.be*
Mari-Andree Vander Elst

A

Accounting, 134–36
Amway, 19, 142
Appointments
  calls and, 75–76
  day planner and, 106–10
  importance of, 77
  Party Plan and, 82
  scheduling, 59
AT&T, 8
Audiotapes, 127, 145–47
Avon, 19

B

Barriers, overcoming, 95–96, 100,
  159–60
Booking skills, 191, 201
Bookings, 76. *See also* Appointments
  day planner and, 106–10
  Party Plan and, 82
  Prime-Time Party Plan and, 165–67
Bookkeeping, 134–36
Building relationships, 34, 46, 95
Business
  control of, 121–30
  growth of, 53–54
  launching, 149, 184–85
  operating, 1–27, 131–37, 138–42
  promoting, 143–49
  record keeping, 133–36
  tips on, 137
Business cards, 132–33

C

Calls
  appointments from, 75–76
  cycle of, 50
  distracting, 123
  equipment for, 140–42
  fear of, 57–58
  follow-up, 45, 52–53, 57–58,
    146–47
  mistakes to avoid, 73

  overcoming reluctance, 78–80
  rehearsing, 72, 75–76
  returning, 124
  techniques, 71–73, 80
Cancellations, 108–9, 160, 162
Career survey, 146–48
Cash traps, 137
Cell phones, 140
Challenges, handling, 126–27
"Checkerboard" development,
  184–86
Christensen, Mary, 218
Citigroup, 8
Closing the sale, 35, 44
Coaching sessions, 154–56, 164
Cold calls, 71–73, 94. *See also* Calls
Commercial breaks, 164–65, 173
Commission, 16–17, 51–52, 58–60
Commitment, 183–84
Communication skills, 41, 55, 126, 189
Company, choosing, 18–20, 62, 125
Competence, 55
Competitive edge, 32, 51
Computers, 138–39
Concern, 55
Conference calls, 141
Confidence, 55, 73, 77, 128
Copier, 139, 140
Courtesy, 55
Critical path, 116–17
Customer base, 53–54, 63–89, 153
Customer files, 87–89
Customer newsletters, 49, 54, 56
Customer service, 48–55, 60
Customers
  desires of, 35
  experience as, 20–22
  keeping, 48–51
  listening to, 31–32, 36–38, 41
  questions for, 37–38
  as recruits, 98–101
  relationship with, 34, 46
  thanking, 46, 49, 61
  treatment of, 40–41